HELPING PARENTS HELP THEIR KIDS

HELPING PARENTS HELP THEIR KIDS

A Clinical Guide to Six Child Problem Behaviors

Ennio Cipani, PhD
California School of Professional Psychology
Fresno

BRUNNER/MAZEL
Taylor & Francis Group

USA	Publishing Office:	BRUNNER/MAZEL *A member of the Taylor & Francis Group* 325 Chestnut Street Philadelphia, PA 19106 Tel: (215) 625-8900 Fax: (215) 625-2940
	Distribution Center:	BRUNNER/MAZEL *A member of the Taylor & Francis Group* 47 Runway Road Levittown, PA 19057 Tel: (215) 269-0400 Fax: (215) 269-0363
UK		BRUNNER/MAZEL *A member of the Taylor & Francis Group* 1 Gunpowder Square London EC4A 3DE Tel: +44 171 583 0490 Fax: +44 171 583 0581

HELPING PARENTS HELP THEIR KIDS: A Clinical Guide to Six Child Problem Behaviors

2 3 4 5 6 7 8 9 0 Printed by George H. Buchanan Co., Philadelphia, PA 1998.
A CIP catalog record for this book is available from the British Library.
⊗ The paper in this publication meets the requirements of the ANSI Standard Z39.48-1984 (Permanence of Paper).

Library of Congress Cataloging-in-Publication Data

Cipani, Ennio.
 Helping parents help their kids : a clinical guide to six child
problem behaviors / Ennio Cipani.
  p.   cm.
 Includes bibliographical references and index.
 ISBN 0-87630-951-1 (alk. paper). —ISBN 0-87630-952-X (pbk.
alk. paper)
 1. Behavior disorders in children—Treatment. 2. Problem
children—Behavior modification. 3. Child psychotherapy—Parent
participation. 4. Mental health consultation. I. Title.
 RJ506.B44C66   1999
 618.92′8914—dc21   98-28099
                                                                      CIP

CONTENTS

Part II
Specific Solutions for Specific Child Problems

PREFACE

Many children demonstrate problem behaviors from time to time, and in many cases parents are able to deal with such problems. Some parents, however, may be at a loss about how to handle certain child behaviors, and they may feel that they have no place to turn. The plethora of parenting books attests to the vitality of the professional field of helping parents. Parenting books or classes frequently either are too general (not providing specific advice for a specific problem behavior) or do not have enough information on how to apply effective techniques in real-life circumstances. You may have heard parents make some of the following comments after attending a parenting class: "That doesn't apply to my child" or I'd like to see someone to do that [technique] with my child!" "I wonder if the instructor could come out and handle my child when she has tantrums and kicks the furniture." If parents have problems dealing with their child's behavior in specific circumstances, should an "expert" be capable of showing them how to handle such problems by addressing the circumstance under which such problems arise? I believe this to be our mission, and I offer this book as a means to such ends for clinicians who work with families.

I have spent many years in the homes of children with severe problem behaviors. In California, the Behavioral Intervention Service, initiated in the late 1970s, has set the trend for providing in home behavioral services to children with disabilities. I have been directly involved in providing such services to families, as well as more recently supervising B.A. and M.A. level personnel who provide such services. This has allowed me to assess the efficacy of behavioral consultation and in vivo parent training programs over hundreds of clients and their families. Recently, I have also extended such a service delivery and technology to children with other disorders who are in foster care or group homes, and to parents who have had their children removed by Child Protective Services and who are attempting to reunify with them. *Helping Parents Help Their Kids* is an outgrowth of almost two decades of experience consulting with families and teaching them how to use specific procedures to deal with their children. I hope that you will find valuable information within these covers.

Some of you who have read other material on behavior therapy or behavioral consultation will notice that this material is devoid of technical explanations. In other words it is not the typical "behavioral" text. If this is your impression, I succeeded in my quest. I intentionally left technical descriptions and behavior analysis terminology out of this book, which may be of some concern to some of the readership. However, the purpose of this book was to communicate with *everyone* who conducts therapy with children and families about simple effective procedures for handling child behavior problems. Many other texts have the effect of leaving the reader lost in technical jargon. Perhaps this technical jargon is getting in the way of making "friends" with people who want to learn effective procedures but do not want to learn a whole new language!

I have given many workshops, and when I explain behavioral procedures in commonsense terms, attendees love this "new" approach or procedure. Actually, it is just a new way of explaining an already existing validated technology. In contrast, workshops that I used to give that involved technical explanations of the procedure had people heading for the door. Let me cite a case in point. In my first year out of Florida State University, 1980, I gave a presentation at a state Council for Exceptional Children (CEC) Conference. The title was something along the lines of "The Effects of Conversational Skills Training on Several Components of Conversation in an Emotionally Disturbed Student." I left the conference room after waiting for 15 minutes for even one person to show up. Several years later (and a lot wiser on my part), I gave a paper at the National CEC titled, "Spare the Rod, Use Behavior Mod." The audience size was around 150 to 170 people, and the attendees for the most part loved the presentation. Since then, I have learned that people will come if you give them a chance to understand and appreciate your knowledge.

This book is for the many people who want to learn new skills. This material is written for you in a user-friendly style. It will not alienate you with a barrage of terms that makes you wonder whether you and I serve the same clientele. I like to think of this book as a bike with good training wheels. The training wheels make you very comfortable as you venture out to learn how to balance the bike and yourself with velocity. I hope this book feels just as comfortable as that bike with training wheels you may have had many years ago.

I also think that people who already have such skills may find a few tricks of the trade they may not have come across, as well as the utility of the clinical forms. In addition, the bibliography will provide the requisite resource material for further study for people who wish to learn more about behavioral consultation. If someone wishes to become even more proficient in some aspect not fully delineated in this book, the reading materials will be of utility.

I truly hope you enjoy *Helping Parents Help Their Kids* and tell a friend (or two). Thank you for entrusting me with some part of your professional education.

ACKNOWLEDGMENTS

The contributions of the researchers cited in the book cannot be over-stated for their pioneering work into empirically validated techniques that benefit families. I am also grateful to the many families I have worked with in shaping my repertoire. They have indirectly taught me how to be a better clinician. I would like to thank Donna Osborne at CSPP for her diligence in typing the manuscript through many revisions. I also like to thank Leah Whitworth, Dr. Jon Bailey, Erika Blinn, and Lucy De Rose for their comments and suggestions on the final draft. Finally, I thank my family for their support and understanding for this undertaking.

INTRODUCTION

"Johnny doesn't listen to his parents."
"Mary is doing terrible at school."
"Time-out doesn't work with our children."
"We can't get Harold to do any of his homework."
"We can't go shopping anymore without a major commotion."
"We have been kicked out of some restaurants in town. It is so embarrassing."

☐ Purpose of the Book

Are some of your cases reflected in the aforementioned hypothetical presenting problems? Are you at a loss as to what to advise parents to do when they are faced with problems like these? Do you feel like some of your cases are in need of something more than dynamic therapy? If so, this book can help.

Helping Parents Help Their Kids was written as a clinical guide for mental health clinicians who provide services to families who have children with behavior problems. As a guide, its three parts address clinical issues in designing and implementing child behavior management plans. In Part 1, three chapters present a general behavioral consultation model. The application of specific behavioral techniques to six problem areas are addressed in Parts 2 and 3. For example, in each of the four chapters that compose Part 2, a specific behavioral technique or program is delineated for child problem behaviors. In the two chapters in Part 3, an empirically tested advice package is presented for multiple problem behaviors that can occur in two different family contexts—shopping trips and restaurants.

Within all of these chapters, the following material is presented:

1. Identification and discussion of child problem behaviors

2. Empirical research studies that validate the efficacy of the behavioral technique or advice package
3. Specific components of the behavioral technique or advice package, using hypothetical scenarios to illustrate implementation
4. Possible questions and other issues parents may have about the specific behavioral treatment

Whereas clinicians can use the first three chapters as a general guide to providing behavioral consultation, the six chapters in Parts 2 and 3 are designed for specific applications. These latter chapters are written in a manner that facilitate easy understanding of the clinical treatment procedures. The easy-to-read style also allows clinicians to use selected chapters as reading material for parents to supplement the therapeutic sessions.

☐ Audience

A primary audience for this book is mental health clinicians. This includes clinical psychologists, family therapists, clinical social workers, psychiatrists, and guidance counselors. *Helping Parents Help Their Kids*, particularly the latter six chapters, is written so that an in-depth understanding of behavioral techniques is not a prerequisite skill. Each chapter attempts to keep technical jargon to a minimum. This is not to say that the presentation is watered down. However, technical jargon can often get in the way of clinicians who want to learn specific behavioral applications but who feel overwhelmed with terminology when they read most material. It is important that clinicians use behavioral techniques in their everyday clinical practice and not necessarily that they be encyclopedias of terminology. To this end, the book strives to present information in a straightforward, nontechnical manner.

Experienced behavioral therapists will also find this book useful. First, the forms that are provided in the Appendix C will aid the clinician in actual clinical practice in terms of data collection, management information, and parent materials. This book will also be of utility to experienced therapists as an adjunct to therapy. Very often, experienced therapists find little or no written material on specific behavioral techniques that is appropriate and applicable for parents to read. Many of the available books are textbooks, which are replete with technical terminology and concepts. The few books that are written in a style more appealing to parents usually present a general behavioral model, which involves the discussion of basic principles and techniques. Less emphasis is placed on specific applications for specific problems. This book utilizes many scenarios to demonstrate a technique or a concept.

A second market is medical personnel who come into contact with families with behavior problems as a part of their professional position. Pediatricians and family practice physicians are often presented with child behavior problems by means of parental reports. *Helping Parents Help Their Kids* can be useful to medical personnel who may seek an intermediate step before outside referral. Again, the book's utility as a clinical guide for specific applications allows medical personnel to provide brief consultation (along with the book as a reading supplement) to these parents. Obviously, if such brief treatment is ineffective in dealing with child behavior problems, outside consultation with an experienced behavioral clinician should be sought.

Finally, this book is applicable for parents as general reading material. Some of the material in the first three chapters may not be applicable or may be more technical in content than needed. However, the specific applications presented in the last six chapters may be relevant for parents. They offer plenty of illustrations and scenarios that demonstrate how to implement the treatment.

☐ How to Use This Book

I recommend that clinicians read the entire book initially. Then, as a particular case presents itself, they should reread the relevant chapter and become reacquainted with such procedures. I also suggest that as therapists begin to detail the specific plan, the book be made available to the parents for their reading. Finally, the forms presented in the Appendix C can be utilized and placed in a file for ready use with families.

A possible use of *Helping Parents Help Their Kids* is to conduct parenting classes for small groups of parents on specific topics, using one of the chapters as the guide. For example, you could run a three-session class (one session per week for a 3 weeks) for parents who have difficulty with their children during family dining outings or who have compliance problems in the home. During September and October, you could run another 3-session class, this one dealing with school-related problems. Each week the parents could be given an assignment—collecting data, designing the strategy, and implementing the strategy. Once again, the forms in appendix C can be useful in guiding parents in these activities. Of course, some parents may need individual sessions to supplement the group parenting class format.

☐ Behavior Therapists Are Not Just Technicians

Throughout this book, an emphasis is placed on the consultation process and its application to specific problem behaviors. However, this does not obviate the need for establishing a positive relationship with the family. Developing empathy and compassion for the family, as well as understanding their unique dynamics, is also of importance. Both sets of skills are necessary.

As a behavior therapist, you must be seen by the family as someone not only who is concerned about the problems they face but also who has the capability to teach them solutions to such problems. Too often, parents visit clinicians who just have empathy for their situation but offer ineffective solutions or no solution at all. These parents may not come away with a positive feeling or hope for their long-term situation. They may eventually come to the conclusion that the best life has to offer them is for them to learn to be more tolerant of their child's behavior (we usually give their child a label to aid them in their quest to develop such tolerance).

Compassion and empathy should be in the repertoire of all behavior therapists. We must never forget that our clients are people who sometimes are in difficult circumstances. Relating to their circumstances, and not minimizing its affliction on them, is a first step. When compassion and empathy for the client's current status in life are supplemented with an effective repertoire for changing child problem behaviors (by teaching parents to become more effective), families get the best of both worlds!

The techniques and procedures presented here are useful in treating commonly referred child behavior problems in families. Children with severe behavioral disorders may require additional, more intense behavioral strategies as well as alternate interventions. Certainly, variations of these strategies for families who have a child with severe problems could be a starting point. However, one may need additional resources or consultation to deal with such problems.

☐ Overview of the Book

In part 1, basic principles of behavioral consultation are covered. The focus of this material is on designing a specific child behavioral plan and teaching the parents to implement that plan. In the Chapter 1, the consultation model is briefly presented and contrasted with a direct services therapy model.

In Chapter 2, five phases of a behavioral consultation model are presented in detail. Contained within this chapter are the following: (1) how to collect data on specific problem behaviors, (2) how to select treatment objectives for child behavior (3) basic principles in designing a child behavioral plan, (4) how to teach parents specific child management skills, and (5) how to collect child progress data and conduct follow-up procedures. This chapter is not intended to cover any of these subjects in great detail, since entire books have been written on these topics. Rather, it is intended as a brief treatment, and the reader is enjoined to consult other sources for more in depth presentation.

Chapter 3, the last chapter in Part 1, provides seven tips and suggestions for clinicians when consulting with parents. These tips and suggestions are not borne out of empirical investigations, but rather personal clinical acumen. They are the result of clinical experience with many cases that seem to have general relevance in consulting.

Part 2 comprises four chapters dealing with four specific techniques that can be used to treat specific child behavior problems or areas. Obviously, a host of other applicable techniques for these problem areas are not covered. Each chapter is not intended to be a complete compendium of all the techniques that could be used to treat specific problem behaviors. Texts that provide coverage for a wide variety of techniques often present a limited explanation of each technique. The approach of this book is to present one technique in great detail. I believed that a book that provides extended coverage on a few select techniques would be of value to many clinicians who need specific detailed instructions and material to guide their efforts to apply the technique correctly in practice.

In Chapter 4, a technique of recent development, behavioral momentum, is presented as a method to treat noncompliance in young children. It is an effective, positive way to get young children to comply with parental requests. As a complement to behavioral momentum, a technique providing a powerful incentive for compliance for older children and adolescents is presented in Chapter 5. Again, these two techniques do not exhaust the possible options for treating child noncompliance. They do, however, provide the clinician with a solid basis to begin treating noncompliance, and the use of such techniques should be successful for many children.

Many families are faced with concerns about their children and school. When the problems become more frequent or severe, clinicians can use a behavioral technique called, the daily report card. It provides parents with some leverage by providing consequences for their child's behavior at school. It requires that the clinician develop a plan and then coordinate the involvement of the parents and school. The last chapter in Part 2,

Chapter 7, presents the effective use of time-out. If you have used time-out and found it to be ineffective, wait! Read this chapter and see whether your understanding and opinions about time-out change.

Part 3, Parent Advice Packages, presents two chapters that address specific areas in which children and families can come into conflict—shopping trips and family outings to restaurants. Unlike Part 2, in which a specific technique was presented for a problem behavior, this part presents a comprehensive advice package for the problem areas. Within the advice package, components and techniques to address a variety of possible child problems that can occur in these settings are delineated. Each advice package was empirically validated in studies conducted at major universities. Clinicians will find these chapters useful when intervening with a variety of problems that can occur when families go shopping or dine out in restaurants with their children.

I

AN OVERVIEW OF CONSULTATION AND PARENT TRAINING

The Clinician as a Consultant

This book presents information on the use of a consultation or technical assistance model in the clinical treatment of child behavior problems and family dynamics. Effective parenting techniques will be identified for general situations, such as school-related problems, playtime, and noncompliance. Advice packages for problem areas or settings, including family shopping trips and family dining out, will also be discussed.

Clinicians who wish to provide technical assistance to parents will find this book helpful. Consultation can be used as a supplement to direct child therapy services. For many clinicians, a consultation model represents a supplement to the existing service delivery procedures that they use. In clinical agencies that favor direct therapy services, consultation may constitute a small portion of their services or may be provided in only a few select cases. Providing consultation (and its preparation of service deliveries) to parents is a decision made on a case-by-case basis. For some clinicians, consultation and technical assistance constitute 80% of the service they provide to many parents.

What are the presenting circumstances that would indicate that a consultation model be used, either as the primary service model or as an adjunct to direct service? Consider a family of three (mother, father, and son). The parents report multiple problems at the dinner table with their son's behavior. He does not come to the dinner table when called. He refuses to eat vegetables, and throws tantrums when told he cannot go play until he has eaten his vegetables. The parents have previously adopted the strategy of taking two Tylenol before dinnertime to "ease their nerves." They report that Tylenol is no longer sufficient.

Although this is obviously a simplified version of an initial interview, the question is, "How does one provide effective services for such a family?" With many therapists, these family problems would be addressed by individual child therapy. The goal would be to have the child gain insight into his behavior. The therapist would focus efforts on getting the child to change these behaviors as a result of their therapeutic contact.

A consultation approach analyzes the family ecosystem at dinnertime and attempts to determine what specific parenting skills or approaches might be developed and used to ameliorate the son's inappropriate and disruptive behavior. The primary tenet of such an approach is that the child's behavior will be changed by changing the parent' behaviors and skills "in vivo." The therapy sessions are used to develop the parenting skills deemed critical in achieving child behavior change. The focus is on changing the parents' behavior to bring about long-term changes in the child's behavior.

☐ Characteristics of the Consultation Model

Two factors characterize a clinical consultation model for child problems:

1. Technical assistance
2. parent education

Technical Assistance Model

A consultation model is a technical assistance model. The clinician provides technical assistance to the parents in specific areas that would affect an identified problem. In a consultation model, the clinician and the parents identify the child behavior problems. Based on the information collected on the identified problems, potential parent management strategies that might address a resolution to the child's problem are identified. The clinician recommends a strategy and obtains the consent and approval of the parents. He or she then teaches the parents to implement such a strategy. The clinician evaluates the efficacy of the selected strategy on the basis of the identified child behavior outcomes. The parents have the primary responsibility for direct service or intervention; the clinician helps them intervene more effectively. In a consultation model, many of the therapy sessions subsequent to the teaching of specific parenting skills involve meeting with the parents to discuss the implementation of the planned program and the child's progress (or lack thereof).

Parent Education Model

The consultation model is also an educational model. Parents are directly taught specific parenting strategies for identified child behavior problems. In some cases, parents are taught how to use a technique already in their repertoire more effectively. For example, the parents with the dinnertime problem described earlier indicate that they use time-out to deal with their son's behavior problems. They describe general scenarios that lead to their use of time-out. Through parental interview, videotape, or real-life observation of parent-child interactions, as well as interviews with the child, the clinician attempts to determine why the use of time-out is ineffective. After collecting this information, the clinician might conclude that time-out is being used inappropriately, such as not being consistently applied toward a specific target behavior, and therefore is rendered ineffective. It is the clinician's job to reevaluate whether time-out, when used appropriately, can be effective in reducing the targeted inappropriate behaviors. If time-out could be effective, the clinician educates the parents on its appropriate use, that is, its consistent application for a specific target behavior. On the other hand, time-out may not be applicable in this case, and the clinician then generates an alternative strategy.

Consultation Versus the Child Therapy Direct Service Delivery Model

There are three major differences between a consultation model and a traditional child therapy approach:

1. Service focus
2. Parental role
3. Length or duration of therapy

Service Focus

In a traditional child therapy approach, the focus is on the individual child manifesting the behavior problems. Treatment is typically rendered through counseling or some other form of direct therapy for the child. In a consultation approach, the service focus is on the family system and, in particular, on requisite parental skills for child management that are needed to bring about change in the targeted problems. Thus, the delivery of services focuses on consulting with the parents about child management skills.

In posing a consultation model for family problems, one might conclude that the parents are the cause of the child's problem behavior. This is a logical but incorrect conclusion of a parent skills training approach. One should not conclude that the parents' skill deficits are the cause of the child's behavior problems. Despite the fact that the clinician may detect the absence of a parent management strategy (and its result on behavior), one cannot verify that such a lack was the original factor in the genesis of this behavior. One can only guess at the original cause of the child's problem behavior. Did the parent skill deficit create the conditions for the problem behavior or did the child's disorder create a parenting style that appears ineffective? This question may not be answerable with our current understanding of behavior. However, it is irrelevant for behavioral treatment strategies. What can be demonstrated in most circumstances is how the lack of certain parenting skills contributes to the maintenance and possible escalation of the child's problems. In other words, worry less about how this situation developed (which cannot be addressed) and more about what to do (given the current circumstance).

Parental Role

In the traditional child therapy approach, the therapist is of utmost importance in delivering the service. The parents' role is either secondary or minimal. The clinician ultimately brings about behavior change in the child through therapy, and the parents are the recipients of this change without being directly involved in the change or its maintenance.

In a consultation approach, the parents play a primary role. It is their behavior (i.e., implementation of the plan) that determines whether the child's behavior changes. The clinician provides technical assistance to the parents by making available a wealth of knowledge on how to manage their child's behavior. Assuming the plan is well designed, it ultimately succeeds or fails on the basis of the parents' ability to implement it.

Duration of Therapy

In traditional approaches, particularly approaches that involve child insight, the duration of therapy can be long. In contrast, in a consultation model (particularly for remediation of specific problems), the length of service is much shorter. The focus is on the remediation of specific identified problems that are currently plaguing the family. This is not to say that the parents learn a generalized parenting skill that will solve all future child behavior problems. If problems occur later, additional consultation and assistance may be needed.

In Chapter 2, specific phases of a consultation model are delineated, and activities within each phase presented.

2

The Five Phases of a Behavioral Consultation Model

The behavioral consultation model, which focuses on targeting specific child behavioral objectives and requisite parenting skills needed to implement a behavioral plan, has the following phases:

1. Gather information and baseline data.
2. Select objectives for intervention.
3. Design behavioral plan.
4. Teach parents specific management skills.
5. Conduct progress evaluation and follow-up.

☐ Phase 1: Gathering Information and Baseline Data

In a consultative approach, the clinician first gathers information and data on the presenting problems. Data collection is an initial clinical activity as well as an ongoing process. The types of data needed during the initial assessment effort range from broad general information to specific rates of targeted problem behaviors.

A caveat is in order. Many people, clinicians included, want to dig right in and read material that presents how-to information. Although reading

---
TABLE 1.   Information model used during assessment

Specific problem behaviors of concern
History of child's behavior
Estimate of rate of behavior
Previous attempts to solve problem
Current strategy used to deal with problem behavior
Baseline rate of problem behaviors

---

about measuring behavior and the methods used to measure behavior may not be exciting, this information is invaluable. Examples and anecdotes are used in the following material to help with application.

Table 1 identifies several types of information needed at this stage of the consultation.

Specific Problem Behaviors of Concern

The first requirement of the data collection effort is to pinpoint the specifics of the problem behavior. Pinpointing specific observable behaviors is done by interviewing the parents, directly observing the child in natural contexts, or both these methods. This can be a difficult process in that parents or referral agents often are vague when presenting the problems of concern.

Clinicians may want to use one of the many behavioral checklists and behavioral rating scales that are commercially available to gain understanding of specific observable child problem behaviors.

Table 2 lists three categories of problem behaviors—compliance problems, other problem behaviors, and other problems not listed—as well as examples of each. Using Table 2, the parents are asked whether their child engages in the behavior. Their response is scored in one of three categories—never (N), seldom (S), or often (O)—and recorded in the first column. The parental responses to the frequency of these behaviors helps the clinician judge the extent of the presenting problems.

Infrequent behaviors may also be a problem, because when the behavior does occur, it creates extreme havoc. Therefore, the parents' perception of the severity of the behavior and an analysis of the potential dangerousness can be an additional factor in determining whether problem behaviors are in need of intervention. In the third column, the severity of the behavior is recorded as high (H) or low (L), as perceived by the parents.

TABLE 2.   List of child problem behaviors

Estimated Level			Behaviors	Perceived Severity	
			Compliance Problems		
N	S	O	Completes activities	H	L
N	S	O	Puts away toys—toys placed back in toy chest, on shelves, or in toy room	H	L
N	S	O	Cleans up room—dirty clothes off the floor or in a hamper; clean shirts and pants hung up or in dresser drawer; garbage in garbage can	H	L
N	S	O	Responds to first request issued	H	L
N	S	O	Independently performs assigned chores	H	L
N	S	O	Complies with "do" commands	H	L
N	S	O	Complies with "don't" commands	H	L
N	S	O	Completes homework	H	L
			Other Problem Behavior		
N	S	O	Interrupts others in conversation—verbally interjects during conversation between two or more people; does not wait for one person to end their conversation; does not say "excuse me"	H	L
N	S	O	Uses verbal profanity	H	L
N	S	O	Is Aggressive against parents	H	L
N	S	O	Is Aggressive against peers	H	L
N	S	O	Is Aggressive against siblings	H	L
N	S	O	Is Aggressive against other adults	H	L
N	S	O	Grabs things from others (without asking)	H	L
N	S	O	Has tantrums—screams, hollers, kicks legs while on floor, whines, kicks or hits property	H	L
N	S	O	Runs in house	H	L
N	S	O	Makes excessive noise; vocalization	H	L
N	S	O	Bosses others	H	L
N	S	O	Destroys own property	H	L
N	S	O	Destroys other property	H	L
			Other Problems Not Mentioned		
N	S	O		H	L
N	S	O		H	L

Note: N = never occurs; S = seldom occurs; O = often occurs; H = high; L = low.

Once the presenting problems are identified, the clinician is ready to have the parents collect data on such behaviors. This activity is called baseline data collection and involves determining the rate of a problem behavior before a behavior plan is implemented. This gives the clinician and the parent the "before" picture of the child's behavior. Baseline data are also used to compare the rate of behavior before and after treatment.

Behavior can be measured in a variety of ways. Some methods may be impractical for parents to use. These methods are often more applicable for university research studies. However, there are several practical ways in which baseline data can be collected by parents:

1. Recording whether an activity or task occurred within a designated time period (*activity occurrence*)
2. Monitoring behavior at spot checks (*spot checks*)
3. Recording the frequency of occurrence (*frequency*)
4. Recording the occurrence or nonoccurrence of behavior within equal intervals (*occurrence/nonoccurrence*)

There are two considerations when selecting a measurement method—the *frequency* and *time duration* the parents will have to collect data. Although frequent and lengthy data collection efforts are obviously more precise than infrequent and minimal efforts, it is often not feasible for parents to collect data often or for an extended period. For example, you may want 7 days of baseline data. However, the parents can reasonably come up with only 2 days. The first maxim in working with parents is for the clinician to try to remain *flexible* in his or her expectations so that clients are not lost because of perceived inflexibility. Flexibility is appreciated by parents and encourages their compliance with treatment plans. Whatever method of data collection is used, it should be designed so that it is feasible for the parents to use.

Activity Occurrence

The first method for collecting baseline data is activity occurrence. It is particularly suited for determining whether a specific activity did or did not occur within a designated period. As a hypothetical example, Mr. and Mrs. F. complain about their daughter Ann's inability to complete her homework in a reasonable time. The clinician might ask them to monitor Ann's homework completion by a target time set at 5:00 P.M. Every day, the parents checked to see if all the homework assigned was completed by 5:00 P.M. The data sheet in Table 3 illustrates the collection of these data for a 6-day period. Mr. and Mrs. F. circled *yes* (homework completed) or *no* (homework not completed) on each date, depending on whether

TABLE 3.   Data sheet for monitoring homework

Date	Homework Completed?	
10 = 3	Yes	(No)
10 = 4	(Yes)	No
10 = 5	Yes	No (none assigned)
10 = 6	Yes	(No)
10 = 7	Yes	(No)
10 = 9	(Yes)	No

Ann completed her homework by 5:00 P.M. The homework was completed 2 of the 5 days it was assigned. With this information, the clinician has a better idea of how often Ann fails to complete her homework.

The data sheet in Table 3 could be adapted for monitoring other activities that are to be completed by a designated time. Another example with a "cleans room" activity is presented in Table 4, with 4 days of data illustrated.

Spot Checks

Monitoring behavior through spot checks is a feasible way of collecting data for some circumstances. In most family situations, the method of monitoring child behavior needs to take into account the necessity of

TABLE 4.   Activity Completion Data Sheet

Child: Rochelle J.
Date: 5/22
Target Activity: Cleans room
Designated completion time: Saturdays before 11:00 A.M.; Wednesdays before 9:00 P.M.

Date	Activity Completed	
Saturday	Yes	(No)
Wednesday	Yes	(No)
Saturday	(Yes)	No
Wednesday	(Yes)	No

TABLE 5.   Spot checks method: Monitoring room cleaning

Child:	Monica
Activity:	Room cleaning
Designated time:	Thursday 3/22 5:00–6:00 P.M.
	Sunday 3/25 9:00–10:00 A.M.

Spot Checks

Day	1	2	3	4	5	6	7	8	%
Thursday	⊕ – +	⊖ ⊕	– ⊕	– ⊕	– +	⊖ ⊕	– ⊕	– + –	6/8 = 75%
Sunday	+ ⊖ ⊕	– ⊕	– +	⊖ +	⊖ ⊕	– +	– +	– + –	4/6 = 67%

running a house as a primary responsibility, with data collection a secondary concern. If the behavior occurs over a period of time—for example, the child is to engage in yard work for a certain length of time—the parents can periodically conduct a spot check to see whether the child is engaged in the activity at the point.

As a hypothetical example, Mr. H. tells the clinician that his daughter, Monica, is to clean up her room on Thursdays between 5:00 and 6:00 P.M. and Sundays between 9:00 and 10:00 A.M. He reports that she seems to take too many breaks and that "not enough cleaning is going on." The clinician asks Mr. H. to randomly spot check during the designated cleaning times to determine whether Monica is engaged in cleaning activities (this would be further defined in specific terms). Table 5 presents the results of his data collection effort.

Mr. H. makes between five and eight *random* spot checks each cleaning time by going to Monica's room and observing whether she is cleaning her room. During each spot check, he watches for a few seconds. If Monica is engaged in cleaning her room, he circles the plus sign in the appropriate column (e.g., spot check 3). If she is not engaged in cleaning her room, he circles the minus sign. At the end of the designated cleaning period, Mr. H. counts the number of spot checks with a plus and compares this number against the total number of spot checks. He then computes a percentage for each day (e.g., 6 of 8 on Thursday, or 75% of time engaged in room cleaning). Maybe the problem is not as bad as Mr. H. originally thought.

Table 6 is another hypothetical example to determine the amount of studying or homework Monica does in her room. In this case, Mrs. H. spot checks her child's studying five times each afternoon, recording whether Monica is studying at the time of the spot check. The percentages reveal that Monica studied between 0% and 40% of the study time during a 4-day period. Some improvement is needed here.

TABLE 6.   Spot checks data sheet

Child: Monica
Activity: Studying
Designated time: 3:00–4:30
Number of random spot checks: 5
Portable oven timer was used to reset spot check interval length.

Date	1	2	3	4	5	%
3/10	+	−	+	−	−	40%
3/11	−	−	−	−	−	0%
3/12	+	−	+	−	−	40%
3/13	−	+	+	−	−	40%

The integrity of the spot check method obviously rests on the unpredictability of the time in which spot checks are conducted. If the child is able to discern a predictable pattern or can see the parent coming, one can imagine the result—the child gets busy at spot checks only. Parents must be clever about spot checking.

Frequency

Collecting frequency data is fairly straightforward. The parent merely records each occurrence of a specific behavior. The frequency counts are then tabulated each day and placed in a summary table. Table 7 illustrates a data sheet for two target child behaviors (tantrums and running in the house). The data collecting system requires the parent to circle the next highest number each time the child either has a tantrum (row 1) or runs through the house (row 2). On April 17, Tom had two tantrums and ran in the house four times.

Occurrence/Nonoccurrence

A final method of measuring behavior involves determining the occurrence or nonoccurrence of a behavior within a number of equal intervals. It is the occurrence/nonoccurrence method of data collection. For

TABLE 7   Frequency data

| Child: | Tom |
| Date: | 4/17 |

	Frequency of Behaviors							
Tantrums	①	②	3	4	5	6	7	8
Running in house	①	②	③	④	5	6	7	8

example, if Mr. S. is monitoring how often his son, Rob, interrupts others at the dinner table, 1-minute intervals can be designated on a data sheet. If Rob interrupts anyone at any point in a given 1-minute interval, the behavior is scored as occurring (by circling O). If he does not interrupt anyone in that interval, the nonoccurrence category is scored (NO is circled). The data sheet in Table 8 illustrates this method in the first 10 minutes of a dinnertime setting.

The data in Table 8 show that Rob interrupts other people's conversation often during dinnertime. On this particular day, he engaged in the behavior at least once per minute for the interval minutes of 1, 3, 5, 6, 8, 9, and 10. The occurrence rate is 70% (a bit high!). This family could use some help.

The design of the data sheet involves specifying the number of equal intervals during which data will be collected. Table 9 provides two examples of data sheets for the occurrence/nonoccurrence method of monitoring a behavior in a 1-hour period. The top represents four 15-minute intervals, and the bottom shows twelve 5-minute intervals. Within each interval, the parent circles O to indicate that the behavior occurred at least once or NO to record that the behavior did not occur.

Table 10 indicates which methods of monitoring behavior might be used for a number of problem behaviors.

History of Child Behavior Problems

The clinician needs to obtain a chronological history of the child's problem behaviors. Interview questions should focus on the following concerns: (1) age of the child when the parents first noticed this type of

TABLE 8.   Equal time intervals

Date:	6/17	
Child:	Rob S.	
Target behavior:	Interrupts others	
Setting:	Dinner table at dinnertime	
Method:	Occurrence (O) /nonoccurrence (NO) over 1-minute intervals, maximum of 20 intervals	

Interval		
1	Ⓞ	NO
2	O	ⓃO
3	Ⓞ	NO
4	O	ⓃO
5	Ⓞ	NO
6	Ⓞ	NO
7	O	ⓃO
8	Ⓞ	NO
9	Ⓞ	NO
10	Ⓞ	NO
	70%	30%

behavior, (2) how long this behavior has been at a problem level, and (3) whether the severity and rate of the behavior have changed across time (i.e., is it getting worse or better?).

Estimated Rate of Behavior

Another set of data that should be collected in the initial session is an estimate of the rate of the problem behaviors. In some cases, this initial estimate of the rate of the identified problem behavior may be the only source of data for judging the level of the problem (i.e., when the parental follow-through on data collection is not good). The parents should be asked to estimate the current rate of each identified problem behavior. Even though this may yield extremely accurate information, it does provide the clinician with some picture of the level of the problem behavior. The following rating scale can be used:

Does the target behavior occur:

• One to 10 times a month?

TABLE 9.   One-hour monitoring system

	15-minute intervals	
1	◎	NO
2	◎	NO
3	○	(NO)
4	◎	NO

	5-minute intervals	
1	○	(NO)
2	○	(NO)
3	○	(NO)
4	◎	NO
5	◎	NO
6	○	(NO)
7	◎	NO
8	○	(NO)
9	◎	NO
10	○	(NO)
11	◎	NO
12	○	(NO)

- One to 10 times a week?
- One to 10 times a day?
- One to 10 times an hour?
- More than 10 times an hour?

Previous Parental Strategies

Information is also needed about previous strategies that were tried by the parents to solve the problem (i.e., what has their response been to such behavior?) and on the efficacy or (lack thereof) of these strategies. There is a specific purpose for collecting such information other than small talk. Gathering detailed information on what strategies have been tried prior to making a treatment recommendation might be the difference between parental adoption or lack of adoption of the new behavior plan. What if a clinician does not collect this information? A conversation similar to that presented below can often ensue:

TABLE 10. Behavior problems and possible methods of monitoring

	Activity	Spot Checks	Frequency	Occurrence Nonoccurrence
Completes assignment	+		+	+
Engaged in assignment		+		+
Puts away toys	+		+	
Cleans room	+	+	+	
Responds to first request issued			+	
Independently performs assigned task	+	+	+	
Interrupts often			+	+
Uses verbal profanity			+	+
Grabs things from others			+	+
Throws tantrums			+	+
Runs in house			+	+
Completes homework	+		+	
Works on homework		+		+
Makes excessive noises; vocalization			+	+

Clinician: I'm going to recommend using time-outs to treat Billy's fighting with his sister . . .

Parent (*interrupts at that point*): Oh, Mrs. Deucey, [*clinician*] we have already tried that. It doesn't work. Billy thinks its a game. We need to try something else.

Clinician Well, I think . . .

Well, I think you're stuck! It is hard to counter the parent's contention that the strategy does not work, even if the clinician suspects it was not implemented correctly. If, however, before recommending time-out, the clinician had the parents present a detailed description of their use of the strategy and detected errors in the design or implementation, the following conversation might have taken place:

Clinician: I think you were on the right track when you thought of using time-out, but for your circumstance, two modifications are going to be needed. First, I recommend (strongly) that you implement time-out whenever Billy hits, or even threatens to hit, his sister. In other words, I want you to catch him sooner than you were previously. Before, you would use time-out after he hit her and she cried (if she did). Now,

TABLE 11.   Previous strategies tried for aggressive behavior

Technique or Discipline Strategy	What Did It Involve?	Was It Effective?	Age
Redirection	Moved him to another activity	No	4
Scolding	Told him he was a bad boy	No	4
Medication	Ritalin	Not Really	5

I want you to keep a close eye on them when they are playing together, and as soon as it looks like he is going to hit—pulls his arm up in a swatting position—I want you to catch his hand right away and take him to time-out, and do this every single time. I mean 90 to 100% of the total times he hits, or attempts to hit, he should go on time-out. Notice how this is different than before. Your vigilance about what Billy and his sister are doing will have to be greatly increased, particularly in the beginning.

Parent: So, you think if we catch him right when it happens, or even before it happens, and do this *every single time,* that time-out will work this time?

Clinician: I think that's the critical difference between what you did before, which didn't work, and what I see as something that has a good chance of working if implemented in this fashion. [*Clinician would continue discussing why this difference is significant*].

Here, the clinician draws the distinction between what was tried previously and what is being recommended now. Making this distinction to the parents can be the difference in their considering adoption versus immediately dismissing the treatment being proposed. Detailed information on what was tried can be an invaluable piece of the initial data set.

A sample set of information from parents is presented chronologically in Table 11. The parents are asked what technique or discipline strategies they tried, what it involved, whether it was effective, and how old the child was when they tried this strategy.

In addition, the clinician needs to gather information on previous contacts with outside professionals, what was recommended by those professionals, and how successful or unsuccessful such consultation was in alleviating the problem behavior.

Current Strategy Used

The clinician also should find out what strategy is currently being used by the parents to deal with this problem. Again, the clinician must ensure that the parents provide detailed information on the current technique for reasons mentioned in the previous section.

As is evident, quite a bit of information needs to be collected before treatment can begin. In brief form, the following hypothetical case illustrates a clinical interview to gather data on a 7-year-old boy named Saul with a referred problem of noncompliance with parental requests.

Parent: He doesn't listen to us at all! I don't know what to do with him. I've tried everything, and it just seems like Saul doesn't respond to me or my husband.

Clinician So you feel Saul is noncompliant with simple as well as complex requests? For example, when you ask him to do something, you have a difficult time getting him to do it. Is that correct?

Parent: Yes. For example, he's a bear in the morning. I can't get him up. And if he comes to the breakfast table, when he gets there, he demands one thing, doesn't eat it, demands something else, doesn't eat that, and yells (at *me*) about the fact that he doesn't like any of the stuff I give him. Once he leaves the breakfast table, it's an extremely arduous task for me to have him dressed in time for school. If he has the TV on, I can't get him away from it. Sometimes I threaten that I won't take him to school if he misses the bus; hoping that will get him going (But I always do anyway.) As you can see, every morning is a struggle. And that's just the morning. Do you want to hear what happens once he gets home from school?

Clinician: It sounds like you have your hands full, but let's get more information on the morning routine before jumping to the afternoon. If it's alright with you, let me just ask you a few more questions about the morning situation and getting Saul ready for school. I need to know how long getting up has been a problem for him.

Parent: It seems like it's always been a problem. I just have a hard time recalling more than a few days when he would get up without constant nagging on my part.

Clinician: What about Saul's being a picky eater and his excessive demanding of food during meals. Has that been a problem for a long time?

Parent: On some days he'll eat something. It depends on whether he's in a good mood. But he just doesn't seem to know how to ask nicely, and it's kind of like living with a grouch in the morning. I've always figured that Saul was not a morning person, but he doesn't seem to be an afternoon person either.

Clinician: Have you tried anything in the past that seems to get him to eat some part of his breakfast?

Parent: Sometimes if I plead with him for a long time, he'll eat a little of his toast or cereal. Some cereals he seems to like more than others.

Clinician: What about getting him up in the morning? Have you found anything that works there?

Parent: Not anything that seems to do it every morning. If I yell and scream at him, eventually he'll wake up, but then, of course, I have to deal with a very cranky child throughout the morning.

☐   Phase 2: Selecting Objectives for Intervention

The information collected in phase 1 leads to the second phase of the consultation—selecting objectives. With the parents, the clinician identifies a list of possible child behavioral objectives for intervention. From this list of possible objectives, the clinician and the parent select one or two initial objectives deemed of higher priority than other identified problem behaviors. These selected objectives are addressed with behavioral plan.

Coming up with the initial child behavioral objectives is a process in which the clinician and the parents reach some form of consensus. The clinician can provide his or her experience in identifying problem behaviors that are in need of immediate attention because of their severity or dangerousness. In some cases, behaviors that are not necessarily dangerous but seem to serve a key role in the triggering of other problem behaviors (e.g., noncompliance) are selected as high-priority objectives.

It is important to initially select only one or two objectives. This might contrast with what the parents desire. The parents may not want to focus on a specific problem but rather want solutions to a wide array of presenting problems (e.g., "What do we do about this, and this, and *this*?". The clinician needs to *delicately* teach the parents that targeting one problem or area at a time is a prudent method. The scenario that follows demonstrates how the clinician offers two initial targeted behaviors with parental input for Saul, 7-year-old boy having difficulty in the morning.

Clinician: There certainly are a lot of areas we can target, Mrs. Smith. However, my approach is to start small and gain control of a few problem behaviors initially. Once we have success with the initial area we select, we can then gradually target other problem areas. I'd like to propose one specific problem area where we could concentrate our effort and see if we can't bring a change in Saul's behavior.

You've mentioned a number of problems during the morning routine as well as problems after school, such as not getting his homework done, watching too much TV, and arguing with his sister. I'd like to suggest that we focus on the problems that are associated with Saul's getting ready for school. This period would seem to be ideal for intervention, since it requires that you initially follow through on a program that lasts for only an hour and a half in the morning. I have found that sometimes it's difficult for parents to implement behavioral plans that occur across the entire day, especially in the beginning. Remember, you'll probably have to change some of the ways you carry out the morning routine, and it's best to learn new routines in small steps. Plans that are to be implemented for specific periods seem to be easier for many parents, as well as being more feasible, given the everyday demands that family life brings on parents. Does that sound reasonable?

Parent: If you say so. It's going to be a monumental task no matter where we start, and I guess you've done this before, so I'm trusting your judgment.

Clinician: Thank you for the vote of confidence! Let's identify the specific problems that occur in the morning. I've pinpointed four areas: first, waking up at a designated time; second; making excessive demands for food items during breakfast; third, not eating the foods requested, and; fourth, getting morning grooming or dressing chores done without significant demanding on your part. Do those four areas sound like a catalog of the problems that you experience in the morning?

Parent: Yeah, that's about it. That seems to describe the problems that occur in the morning.

Clinician: I'd suggest that we target just these problems—Saul's excessive demanding of different foods and his not finishing breakfast. I would like to leave the other two problem areas alone for a few weeks so that we can focus our efforts on these two objectives. Of course, we would address the other problems at some later point once we can get a handle on these problems. Does that sound reasonable to you?

Parent: Sounds good to me. Let's start somewhere!

Clinician: Okay, let's plan how we're going to manage Saul's behavior during the morning.

In most cases, the clinician's suggestions are acceptable to the parents as a starting point. In a few cases, however, the parents may be vehement about needing help on a problem area that is of critical concern to them. If the parents think that another problem area needs to be addressed immediately, the clinician should become an interested listener. Depending on the intensity of their desire and the rationale for their choice, the clinician might judge that it is best to be flexible and target their choice.

The scenario that follows picks up after the clinician has offered her rationale and selection for targeting objectives in the morning and illustrates her flexibility.

Parent: I know we've talked a lot about the problems that occur in the morning, but there's a problem that's of grave concern to me. Saul is doing poorly at school. He's sent to the principal's office regularly, and I'm afraid he's eventually going to be expelled. I've talked with his teacher, and she doesn't know what to do. I *really* need help with his problems at school. While his behavior at home is troublesome, I'm worried that he'll eventually drop out of school when he gets older because it's been such a disastrous experience for him.

Clinician: I can see how this is of grave concern to you. I agree that Saul's behavior at school seems to be pointed in the wrong direction. Let me find out more about what problems are occurring at school. In addition to to our discussion here, I'll also need to talk with his teachers to get a more accurate picture of his school day, with your consent, of course.

☐   Phase 3: Designing a Behavioral Plan

Once the objectives have been selected, the clinician needs to design the behavioral plan or strategy that will be used to address the child's behavioral objectives. The clinician draws on the information collected during the data gathering phase to determine which strategy (or strategies) would seem to be most effective in changing the desired target behaviors. A behavioral plan attempts to systematically change the parent-imposed consequences for the child's behavior. The consequence for the problem behavior has to be altered—for example, not giving the child a cookie while he or she is having a tantrum. Also, the consequence for not throwing tantrums is altered, such that the child earns cookie (or something else) when he or she does not display the targeted behavior for some period of time.

In some cases, it is clear that the problem behavior occurs as a result of parent reaction to the behavior. If the clinician is able to discern this, determining the strategy to use is more straightforward. The example that follows illustrates how the clinician rearranges the parental consequences of misbehavior after treatment.

Before treatment

Child misbehavior occurs → desired parental response

After treatment

Child misbehavior occurs → desired parental response not given

Consider the following four cases that illustrate an obvious relation between the child's problem behavior and the parental response.

Case A. Brian, a 6-year-old boy, goes to the supermarket with his mother. Once inside the store, he sees some cookies he wants and asks his mother, "Mommy, can I have those cookies? Can you buy them for me?" His mother responds by saying. "Well, maybe I'll get them later, but right now I need to get some more groceries so we can have dinner tonight." As his mother pushes the shopping cart away from the cookies, Brian begins to cry and whine, "But I want the cookies. You have to buy me the cookies. Mommy, mommy!" His mother stops the cart, turns back, picks up the cookies, and puts them in the shopping cart. Of course, Brian stops crying and whining, which makes his mother more likely to give in next time when crying and whining occur.

In this example, the appropriate behavior (asking for the cookies) did not result in Brian's getting the cookies. However, throwing a tantrum did produce the desired results. What he is learning is, "Ask nice and I get put off, but scream, whine, and throw a tantrum, and that gets Mommy's attention—pronto!" If you were Brian, and you really wanted those cookies, what would you do—ask nicely or scream? The answer is painfully obvious.

When the clinician spots this relation between child misbehavior and getting cookies, he or she suggests an alternative method of dealing with two sets of behavior—tantrum behavior and nontantrum behavior. The clinician would recommend that if Brian throws a tantrum, no cookies are given. He or she would also recommend that if he doesn't throw tantrums that cookies are then given. The parental consequences have been altered for both tantrum and nontantrum behavior.

Case B. Bobby's father has some yard work to do. He calls Bobby over and says, "I need you to use the blower and sweep away the leaves from the driveway." Bobby, who has been playing basketball, does not move right away. On seeing Bobby's lack of enthusiasm for getting to the requested task, the father yells, "Bobby, I meant *now!*" Sensing urgency in his father's voice, Bobby goes to the garage and gets out the blower. He plugs the extension cord into the wall and begins to blow the leaves away from the driveway. At the same time, Bobby's brother, Billy, is told by his father to dig up three plants that have died and place the remains in the garbage can. Billy agrees, and his father walks away. However, after getting the shovel, Billy lies on the grass and postpones the task of digging up the plants. Bobby finishes his task and puts away the blower. At that time, his father returns to the backyard and sees that Bobby is finished and says, "Good job. The driveway looks very good. Now I'd like you to come over here and help me paint the fence." Meanwhile, Billy still has not pulled out the first dead plant and continues to putter around instead of getting to work. A half hour later, Bobby's father says, "Okay, that's about enough yard work for today. Let's go eat. We'll finish the rest another day."

It is not hard to see how Bobby will eventually learn that doing work does not pay off and will begin to engage in the same off-task behavior as his brother Billy. To reinforce compliance, task completion should not result in additional work while failure to complete the task results in the postponement and avoidance of work. Nevertheless, this scenario gets played out in many homes every day. The clinician realizes this mistake in parental response to both sons and proposes to teach the father a different way of conducting yard chores. The father is to assign each child a task of comparable level, and when that task is done, the child is finished. If the boy lags, he stays until it is done. Under these conditions, Bobby would have finished early and Billy would still be outside until he removed the dead plants.

Case C. Shelly, a 4-year-old girl, is entertaining herself in the playroom with her dolls. Her father is sitting on the couch reading a newspaper. Shelly calls out to her father multiple times to watch as her dolls talk to each other in a play fantasy. The father ignores her until she throws one of the dolls and it hits the wall. The father then pleads with Shelly not to do that again.

In this scenario, the behavior that gets attention is not the right one, and it is not appropriate attention getting. In this case, the clinician would determine that appropriate play should receive the father's attention and would teach the father to intermittently attend to Shelly during play, such as asking her to explain what she is doing with her dolls. Concurrently, the father would use some form of time-out (see Chapter 7 for details) when play is inappropriate (e.g., throws dolls against the wall).

Case D. While dining out with his parents, Jose can sit still at the dining table, waiting for the food, for about 5 to 10 minutes. If this premeal time goes beyond this limit (and it is usually about 30 minutes), however, Jose typically darts under the table, plays inappropriately with

TABLE 12. Contingency

Appropriate behavior occurs → Access powerful reinforcer
Problem behavior → Powerful reinforcer becomes unavailable for some time

the utensils or runs away from the table. It becomes obvious to the clinician that Jose is not capable of sitting when the premeal time is longer than 10 minutes.

In this case, the clinician would attempt to gradually increase the length of time Jose could sit at the dining table, from 5 to 10 minutes to 20 to 25 minutes over a number of dining-out experiences (see Chapter 9 for specifics). The target goals, in increments, might be the following:

Phase A: Can sit at dining table while engaged in premeal activities for 3 to 8 minutes

Phase B: Can sit at dining table while engaged in premeal activities for 10 to 12 minutes

Phase C: Can sit at dining table while engaged in premeal activities for 12 to 16 minutes

Phase D: Can sit at dining table while engaged in premeal activities for 15 to 20 minutes

Phase E: Can sit at dining table while engaged in premeal activities for 15 to 25 minutes

In some cases, it may not be immediately apparent to the clinician what parental responses are the reason for the child's misbehavior. In these cases, the clinician attempts to reduce the problem behavior by selecting a powerful reinforcer for the parents to use when appropriate behavior occurs. Concurrently, this powerful reinforcer becomes unavailable when the problem behavior occurs. Table 12 is a general schematic depiction of the contingency.

Many of the programs delineated in the following chapters attempt to increase appropriate behavior by presenting powerful reinforcers when such behaviors occur. How does one determine what a powerful reinforcer is? Reinforcers are often best determined by the child when asked to list things or activities he or she would like to earn. If one is still in doubt, money contingencies usually are effective in producing changes in appropriate behaviors—that is, the child earns money for appropriate behavior (at some designated level). The child could then spend money to buy things or activities he or she wants. If money is used as a powerful reinforcer, the parent must make sure that the child cannot get money for misbehaving. An example of using money for appropriate behavior is illustrated in Table 13.

TABLE 13.   Example of powerful monetary reinforcer for desirable behavior

Target Behavior:
Interrupting others during dinner [would be defined]

Consequence for desirable behavior during dinner
    Interval of not interrupting—5 cents
Consequence for target behavior during dinner
    Intervals of interrupting—0 cents
Back-up reinforcer for money
    50 cents needed to earn special dessert
    and half hour of extra TV time

Points can be used in a similar fashion to money. Points can also be awarded for appropriate behaviors and not given when the target problem behavior occurs. The points are then traded in at some future time by the child for backup reinforcers. The behavioral plan in Table 14 uses points as the consequence for desirable and undesirable behavior.

In the plan in Table 14, the child gets 4 points for a positive or complimentary statement toward his sister. This will provide an incentive to engage in that behavior to get access to video games (or backup reinforcers for points). He needs at least 30 points to get 30 minutes of video game time. Engaging in verbally abusive statements or criticism toward his sister, however, results in a loss of 2 points from his total. This removal of points is called a *cost response* (featured in Chapter 5).

Once the clinician has mapped out the behavioral plan, he or she needs to present and sell it to the parents. Briefly, a clinician might present a

TABLE 14.   Point system for positive and abusive statements

Targeted behavior:
Verbally abusive statements and verbal criticism toward sister [would be defined].

Consequence for desirable behavior
    Complimentary or positive
    statements toward sister—4 points
Consequence for undesirable behavior
    Verbally abusive statements or criticism toward sister—loss of 2 points
Backup reinforcers for points
    30 points—30 minutes of video games after 6:30 P.M.
    40 points—45 minutes of video games after 6:30 P.M.

behavioral plan to the parents of Saul, the 7-year-old child with problem behaviors in the morning as follows.

Clinician: As we established in the last session, we're going to attempt to increase Saul's motivation to get up on time and groom and dress himself without constant reminders or interferences on your part by implementing a behavior plan that you'll carry out. Using this type of approach, I've found that a child's behavior changes when the parents are taught a new way of dealing with the behavior. This is in contrast to what many peoples' conceptions of therapeutic services are or should be. Many people believe that behavior problems in children should be addressed by a professional who meets with the child on a regular basis to discuss his or her problems. However, in our consultative approach, we view you, the parent, as the key ingredient for success in changing child behavior. It is our job to determine what additional strategies you might employ that will lead to success. Is this conception of service delivery different from what you had initially perceived?

Parent: Well, to be honest, I wasn't sure what we would do. He has been to counseling before, and that didn't seem to work. He did like going to the counseling sessions, but whatever they talked about in there didn't seem to spill over in terms of his behavior at home. So, I guess if anything is going to change, we're going to have to do something at the time he and I have the conflicts.

Clinician: I'm sorry to hear that your previous experience with counseling wasn't the solution, but it looks like you've come to the conclusion that you need to try something else. Seven years of age is a good time to develop a behavior plan to begin to change Saul's behavior in the home environment. As he gets older, it may become increasingly difficult for you to deal with his inappropriate behaviors. So, I'm glad we're at this juncture of deciding to modify his behavior by systematically implementing a behavioral plan.

Parent: Yes, I realize that as Saul gets older, given the way things are going now, I'll have less control. It worries me sometimes when I think that I'll have virtually no impact on his behavior when he's a teenager if I can't get him to listen to me when he's 7 years old.

Clinician: Let me tell you what I think we should do to change his behavior during morning routine. We're going to use a behavior plan called Grandma's Rule. The Grandma's Rule maxim is "You don't eat your dessert until you've finished your vegetables!" You've probably heard that before, haven't you? The relationship grandma designed between eating vegetables and then getting dessert can be used for other problem areas as well. For example, if you don't get certain things done, you don't get to play. On the other hand, when you complete certain things, you get to go play. We can use Grandma's Rule in the form of a behavioral plan, which will require your son to get up and get his chores done before being able to watch TV or play Nintendo in the morning. Let me get into the specifics of the plan.

☐ Phase 4: Teaching Parents Specific Management Skills

Once the behavioral plan has been delineated to the parents and they verbally commit to implementing it, the clinician needs to present the specific requisite skills needed to implement the plan. This specific parenting skills–training approach needs to be distinguished from a general parenting class. In the latter, the parents are taught about basic principles of parenting. They often then have to develop their own plan of attack based on what they learned. Parents often say that general parenting classes lack specifics. In the parenting skills–training approach, the emphasis is on the clinician's developing a specific behavioral plan tailored to the family's needs and experiences. The clinician then teaches the specific parenting skills that are needed.

The specific parenting skills–training approach delivers training through a variety of techniques. The clinician can use verbal instruction, a written behavioral plan delineating the specifics, video modeling, role-play modeling, and direct observation of the parent in the home with feedback (if possible). Role playing is an effective way to demonstrate the specific performance of the parenting skill being developed in a therapy session. Below is an example of a session teaching the parent how to use the behavioral chart for tracking the child's compliance with the morning routine. After the clinician explains the plan, they role play, with the clinician serving as the child.

Clinician: As we discussed last time, Saul will have to complete his morning dressing and grooming skills, as well as get up on time, to earn time either watching TV or playing Nintendo before the bus picks him up. I have designed a chart to help you implement this plan [Table 15]. The chart helps identify the morning requirements and the sequence in which they should be performed by your son.

As you can see, for each day, each time a task is completed, Saul places a check next to that task in the "Completed" column. You would verify that this task was actually completed by initialing his check. Once all the checks have been placed for each of the tasks and you have verified

TABLE 15.   Chore chart example

Date: _____

Chores	Completed?
1. Gets up within 5 minutes	_____
2. Toilets self	_____
3. Grooms self	_____
4. Dresses self	_____

this with your initials, Saul would eat breakfast. Contingent on finishing breakfast (however you define "finishing"), he then gets to have up to 25 minutes of TV or Nintendo if all the checks and breakfast are completed before 7:15 A.M. The incentive for Saul is that he would be able to have 25 minutes of TV and Nintendo time before departing for the school if he complies with the tasks for the morning routine. Remember, however, it is important to *not* allow him to play Nintendo or watch TV before all his tasks are completed and his breakfast eaten. If he doesn't complete all the tasks, he isn't able to watch TV or play Nintendo at any point in the morning.

We also specified a fail-safe criteria that would require you to physically help him complete the tasks if 7:15 arrived and one or more of the tasks had not been completed. This ensures that Saul does manage to get on the bus to go to school each day. If the fail-safe criteria are reached, you would help him, but he would not earn the reinforcer. That should motivate him on subsequent mornings, remembering that he will miss out if he gets lazy. Does that sound about right to you?

Parent: Yeah, that's it. Do I get any practice at this before I actually have to use it with my son?

Clinician: Yes, let's role play. I'll play your son, you be you, and we'll see if you can implement that chart system and provide the appropriate consequences to him. You will indicate to me what you would do when I complete the task and what you would do when I do not complete the task. Of course, I won't brush my teeth or dress myself here, but let's say that I either do it or don't do it, and let's see what your response is."

Patient: Okay, fire away!"

Clinician: Let's say I go to the bathroom and come back and claim to have brushed my teeth. I begin to put a check in the completion column, but you notice that the toothbrush is dry. What would you do?

Patient: I would not verify the check, and if that task is not completed to my satisfaction, then he doesn't get Nintendo. He has to complete the task to my satisfaction before 7:15 to get Nintendo. I would also tell him at that point that his toothbrushing was not satisfactory and to get busy.

Clinician: Good, that's the way to handle it. But let's say I start arguing with you and say that you're a liar and that I did brush my teeth, and how would you know that I didn't brush my teeth because you weren't there.

Parent: I would, as we had talked about, restate my finding and the consequence for not brushing your teeth. I would also restate what you need to do to get a check verified by me for that task. The decision is yours!

Clinician: Good! You catch on quick!

For two-parent families, both parents must commit to the behavioral plan. Obviously, if one parent is implementing the plan and the other is not, the desired effects on child behavior become less probable. As a clinician, you will have to discern if an inconsistency in implementation between the two parents is due to an error in understanding (a fixable problem) or some other dynamic between the couple. If it is the latter case, such a problem needs to be addressed immediately if possible, before the plan is put into place. It is not the intent of this book to discuss how to uncover marital relationship issues that can affect the implementation of the behavioral plan. The neglect of this topic is not due to its relative importance. Rather, since such issues have been treated more extensively in other material, the reader is enjoined to consult those readings.

☐ Phase 5: Progress Evaluation and Follow-Up

An important tool of any behavioral plan are timelines to evaluate the efficacy of the plan and follow-up consultation. To be effective, consultation usually requires follow-up of the case over time. The failure of one-shot consultation deals in which the clinician presents information or advice to the parent for one session is well-known to behavior therapists. It is important for the clinician to follow-up with the parents after their implementation of the behavioral plan.

Follow-up sessions should involve reviewing and monitoring data on the child's behavior. The clinician examines the data to determine whether the plan is feasible and effective or whether it needs to be revised. The clinician discusses his or her analysis of such data with the parents during follow-up sessions. The clinician also checks whether the parents are having any further difficulty and if they are pleased with their child's progress and behavioral plan. Reviews of progress sessions are more frequent in the beginning and, with success, become less frequent as the need to review data and provide information to the parents becomes less imperative.

During follow-up sessions, information on the following four areas are obtained: (1) child progress on behavioral objectives, (2) parental implementation of behavioral plan, (3) development of additional child behavioral problems, and (4) parental concerns relating to the current plan or the child's progress.

As an example of a follow-up consultation to evaluate the progress of Saul in complying with his morning tasks, Saul's mother meets with the clinician after plan implementation and presents data on the effectiveness of the plan. Review of the data indicates that the behavioral plan resulted in some increase in compliance to most of the tasks. However, the clinician notes that on 2 of 5 days, Saul failed to dress himself in time and subsequently did not earn the reinforcer. The following conversation illustrates how the clinician might probe for information to determine how the plan might be revised to resolve the dressing problem.

Clinician: Okay, it looks like you're reporting that Saul is having difficulty with the dressing chore on some days, and the data seem to bear this out. Is that correct?

Patient: "Yes, on some days it's just difficult for him to get dressed. Maybe it's the type of clothing that he's wearing at the time.

Clinician: Would there be anything in particular about the clothing he is to wear on those days? Is it too tight? Does it require zipping something? Does he have trouble with getting some part of his clothing on?

Patient: Yes, he seems to have trouble when he has to put a sweater over his shirt when the weather is cold. We're just getting into the fall season, so some days he needs to wear a sweater and other days he doesn't. And that seems to cause him problems.

Clinician: Okay, that's good information. Let's see if we can handle it in a different way to make the plan more successful. I'd like to revise the plan in the following manner. When you're requiring him to wear a sweater, how about if we provide a little help to him on those days. Tell him that if he has trouble putting on his sweater he can just ask you to help him with the sweater. If you help him get the sweater on, let's go ahead and count that as a completed task without your helping him being an issue, for the sweater only. Let's implement that for a couple of weeks and see if that solves the problem. If it does, that's great and we can proceed to other problem areas. If it doesn't, then we know that it wasn't necessarily the problem with the sweater, but possibly some other motivational issue and we'll deal with it at that time. How does that sound to you?

Patient: That sounds like a workable plan, and now that I think about it, I probably should have thought of that before. This has been very helpful, and I can't wait to see how you're going to advise me in terms of problems that we have after school. Some of the problem areas have been getting better, but in other cases he doesn't seem to be gaining any insight to his problem.

Clinician: Well, let's get this problem area pretty well under control and then see if we can't teach him appropriate behaviors and insight for those times after school.

☐ Summary

In a consultation approach, the clinician attempts to pinpoint specific child behaviors that are at problem levels and then designs a behavioral plan for the parents to implement that addresses specific child behavior objectives. The parents are then taught specifically how to implement the behavioral plan. The clinician follows up on the child's progress toward the plan's objectives and modifies the plan if needed. In Chapter 3, suggestions and tips for using a consultation model are presented from the clinician's perspective.

Suggestions and Tips for Consulting With Parents

The general model for providing consultation to parents for treating child behavior problems in home and community settings, delineated in Chapters 1 and 2, seems fairly straightforward. However, the simplicity involved in consulting with parents on such problems is deceptive. After all, if it were simple, would there not be just a few rare instances in which children drove their parents to frustration? In reality, many families find themselves at a loss for dealing effectively with their children, even after professional involvement. What factors are critical in achieving child behavior change? Parental follow-through and adherence to the behavioral plan are often the keys to success.

How does a clinician increase the likelihood of the parents' successfully implementing the behavioral plan? The difference between successful implementation and failure can often be traced to the process used in a given case. The probability of parental follow-through can be greatly enhanced by implementing a number of components in the consultative process.

Eight factors are involved with successful implementation. These tips and suggestions, the result of years of clinical practice in consulting with parents, are as follows:

1. Consultation is not quick-fix advice giving.
2. Don't bite off too much.
3. The problem behavior didn't just happen yesterday, so don't expect it to go away tomorrow.

4. Prepare parents for the "extinction burst"—things getting worse before they get better.
5. Implementing child behavior management plans is not a part-time responsibility.
6. The focus on increasing appropriate behavior rather than just decreasing problem behavior.
7. Get the necessary parental follow-up through for success.
8. Balance the needs (and requirements) of the behavioral plan with the needs of the family.

☐ Suggestion 1: Consultation Is Not a Quick Fix

A tendency for some clinicians is to attempt to solve a presented problem behavior right on the spot. This is "quick-fix advice" in contrast to consultation. Plenty of people give quick-fix advice to parents on child-rearing approaches, but consultation involves a much more through understanding of the nature and severity of the problem behavior. Responsible behavioral consultants do not give quick-fix advice.

In consulting with parents, it is easy to fall into the trap of giving quick-fix answers. The tendency to offer advice on the spur of the moment is often occasioned by the parents' lament, "We need something to try tonight! We can't take another night with Raul screaming like he does." The clinician feels the need to relieve these parents' suffering at once. Novice clinicians might be tempted to say, "Oh, that's easy to solve. I've seen this type of problem before and it's fairly simple. Here's what you need to do." The clinician may advocate in this case that the parents ignore Raul when he screams. He tells the parents that Raul is screaming to get their attention and that when they attend to him, they are reinforcing this screaming behavior. Sounds good! What can go wrong? Plenty! What happens in the next (second) session when Raul's parents, Mr. and Mrs. D., come back a week later?

Clinician: Well, Mr. and Mrs. D, did you ignore Raul when he began to scream?

Mrs. D: Well, we did most of the time. But one time, Raul screamed so loudly, I thought he was going to lose his voice. I gave him ice cream to soothe his throat. It seemed like he was getting worse because we were ignoring him when he screamed. So my husband and I decided to ignore him if it wasn't a loud scream. If it was a loud scream, we wouldn't let that go on. We also think Raul might need medication to help him settle down.

Clinician (to himself) Oh no, How could they have fouled this up?

Providing consultation to parents about behavioral plans is not a simple and easy proposition. In this scenario, the clinician experienced the result of giving quick-fix advice. There are two things that often go awry with quick-fix advice leading to unsuccessful attempts at child behavior change.

First, the clinician can offer an approach with an insufficient amount of detailed information about the nature, circumstances, and severity of the screaming. Hence, the devised plan may be inappropriate for the circumstances. This becomes a more distinct possibility the less information the clinician collects about the nature and characteristics of the problem behavior, the child, and the family. The previous two chapters are at the beginning of this book for a reason. It is essential to first gain a full understanding of the problem behavior and the social environment in which it occurs.

Second, quick-fix advice can result in poor implementation of the advice by the parents, which results in lack of child behavior change. In the example just given, a thorough interview may have produced information that would have led the clinician to realize that Mr. and Mrs. D. would not be prepared to deal with an "extinction burst" in which behavior initially gets worse before it gets better. Unless preparation for such a likelihood was laid out by the clinician, the resulting extinction burst can spell disaster for continued implementation.

The clinician might have handled the parents presentation of their child's problem differently; as shown here.

Mr. D.: Our 6-year-old son, Raul, is out of control! He drives my wife and me crazy. We need something we can do tonight to give us some hope, some relief. [*Mr. D. goes on to delineate all kinds of behavior problems with Raul.*]

Clinician: It sounds like you have terrible a situation on your hands. I can certainly understand your urgency. But before we design a plan together to address Raul's problems, I'm going to need to gather a lot more information. It sounds like a really tough situation, and I can understand why you may have had a difficult time trying to come up with a discipline plan to resolve this. My hat's off to you for your effort and resilience alone. [*Note the contrast between this scenario claiming that presenting problems are tough and the previous clinician's claim that they are easy.*] Let me gather some basic information, and together we'll devise a plan that, given the information gathered, looks like it might succeed. Before implementation of that plan, I'll prepare you to implement it and anticipate possible impediments to implementation. We'll set implementation and success dates, and we'll monitor the effectiveness of our plan on a regular basis.

This clinician is laying the foundation for a systematic approach to solving the presenting problem and is not offering an on-the-spot answer. Consultation involves collecting information, analyzing the nature of the problem and its social environment, training the parents on the designated support plans, mentally preparing them for implementation, and systematically monitoring progress of the plan and the child. The clinician must resist the temptation to give quick-fix advice on the spur of the moment.

☐ Suggestion 2: Don't Bite off Too Much

A family may present numerous child behavior problems, all needing intervention. Once again, this invitation gets the professionals' engines rolling and they tend to want to appear omnipotent and solve all the behavior problems presented. Many clinicians fall into this trap out of their sincere desire to assist families in dire need of such help. They empathize with the family situation and call on powerful technology to change wrong to right, to bring happiness where there is disharmony, and to ride off into the sunset knowing they have changed the lives of people for the better! Right? Not quite! The movies are not to be confused with real life. Children with behavior problems do not just wake up one morning and walk down the path of righteous behaviors for the rest of their lives, solely because of something the clinician does the day before. Long-term problems require long-term involvement (at least longer than a 1-day consultation). Multiple child behavior problems need to be addressed in a systematic fashion.

When the clinician attempts to solve multiple problems simultaneously, he or she may be biting off too much. When you bite off too much, your mouth is so full you can't swallow. Therefore, taking smaller bites is obviously more conducive to easy swallowing. The analogy for this in parent consultation is not to set up numerous behavioral plans for multiple problems in the beginning session.

The attempt to solve multiple child behavior problems all at once creates two conditions that can be barriers to eventual success: (1) the plan may be too complex to follow, and (2) the plan may require too much parental behavior change. First, such programs tend to be extremely complex to follow. In some referrals, previous reports attempt to address eight or nine problem behaviors with eight separate behavioral plans. Can anyone not see why these plans are destined to fail? Professionals are to be dissuaded from setting up a plan that has so many intricacies that one needs to design a computer expert system to keep track of what child behavior results in what parental response. Second, not only is it impractical from a memory standpoint to expect implementation of numerous plans by parents, but it also usually is physically and logistically difficult for parents to carry out such a plan.

The danger of attempting to implement a complex behavioral plan for a child with numerous problem behaviors who has a long-standing history of such problems can be seen in the following interview scenario.

> A clinician identified, through the initial interview, several behavior problems with Robin, the 7-year-old daughter of Mr. and Mrs. F.: (1) Robin throws tantrums frequently when denied access to something (i.e., a toy, an object, or an event) she had requested; (2) she destroys her brother's toys when upset; (3) she acts aggressive against her younger brother; (4) she is frequently noncompliant with parental requests to clear off her part of the dinner table; and (5) she has difficulty getting chores done in the morning in a reasonable time frame without constant pleading from her mother. The clinician decides to design five different behavior programs to address each of these problem behaviors individually. After 2 hours of discussion delineating the program and contingencies to the parents, the clinician asks Mr. and Mrs. F. if there are any questions. Mr. and Mrs. F. respond, "Yes, can you begin at the beginning? We aren't sure what we are going to do about Robin's tantrums."

Implementing five different behavioral plans would be difficult logistically, let alone remembering the different plans for different behaviors.

A second important reason to resist the urge to solve multiple problems immediately is the inability to change many parental behaviors. Changing the child's behavior may often be fairly straightforward, but changing the parents' behavior is the more difficult task. Parents have practiced their responses to the child's problem behaviors for months (even years). Even though they may know that they are not reacting correctly to their child's misbehaviors, they are likely to repeat their incorrect reactions in the future. If the clinician realizes this tendency for the parents to react as usual to misbehavior, it is easier to understand why the behavioral plan should focus on a smaller subsection of the totality of problems: it must be designed to be within the parents' current capacity for change in their response pattern. It is not easier to change the parental response pattern to one set of behaviors that occur in a certain period than to attempt to change their response pattern for seven or eight different behaviors that occur constantly across the waking hours of the day? Setting up a limited behavioral plan also teaches the parents that creating the conditions in which the child's behavior will change involves a systematic change in their behavior in small, easy-to-learn steps. It is better to be completely successful in one area than 50% successful in eight areas. For best results, the clinician and parents should take it one step at a time.

The earlier scenario would play differently if the clinician tried to work with the parents on designing a smaller, more workable behavioral plan.

Clinician: Okay, Mr. and Mrs. F., you have collected data on five inappropriate behaviors that Robin exhibits, and all seem to be in need of intervention. Our goal will be to decrease their frequency of occurrence. It seems that two behaviors, destroying her brother's toys and hitting her brother, happen in the same circumstances—during playtime. I suggest that we target this circumstance and develop a behavioral plan to deal with Robin's inappropriate behaviors during playtime. This plan will also provide an incentive program for Robin to play cooperatively with her younger brother and to avoid situations that often lead to her hitting him or destroying his toys. This will require you to implement the designed plan during these play periods only. How does that sound so far?

Mrs. F.:   Sounds great! I think it's important to go after playtime. I believe we can also increase our vigilance of Robin's behavior during certain selected times. It sounds a lot better than having to follow her around all day!

☐ Suggestion 3: The problem behavior didn't just happen yesterday, so don't expect it to go away tomorrow.

This is a corollary of suggestion 2. One of the most important lessons the clinician can teach parents is that a child behavioral plan does not bring about dramatic reductions in the problem behavior in one day. Rather, the influence of the behavioral plan usually is demonstrated over time. This is an important lesson because when faced with an increase in a problem behavior, many parents immediately resort to another intervention. They employ a "crisis approach" to problem behavior: when the behavior is bad or gets worse, they do something else. This is why a clinician may hear parents say, "We've tried everything." What this often means is that with each new crisis of behavior outburst, the parents dump what they were currently doing and try something else. Therefore, a single strategy has not been used during a sufficiently long period.

Why do parents expect an intervention to solve all the child's problems (as well as theirs) instantaneously? This is largely due to misconceptions about child behavior change. Too often, parents are under the impression that children will change their behavior once they gain "insight" into why they do what they do. Under this model, a child's behavior would change across the board once this insight is achieved (i.e., the "light goes on"). Decades of research and clinical practice, however, have shown that behavioral plans usually need time to influence behavior.

Parents should be taught that, with the implementation of an effective behavioral plan, the child's behavior will usually change gradually. They will notice that the time intervals between the problem behavior and its next occurrence will get longer. In the first several days, however, it is possible that the rate of problem behavior may actually get higher (see suggestion 4). The parents need to content themselves with small changes in behavior each day, with the overall level going down (as desired) in the long term. If changes in inappropriate behavior happen quickly, parents should count their blessings. But they shouldn't expect this. Such an expectation can interfere with long-term implementation of a behavioral plan.

☐ Suggestion 4: Prepare parents for the "extinction burst"—Things getting worse before they get better.

The following hypothetical scenario is of an interview after the parent implemented time-out the previous week.

Parent: Dr. B., we tried time-out, but it didn't work. Sarah really *screamed,* and I thought she was going to pass out. I pleaded with her not to scream in time-out since it was upsetting her. She didn't listen. Two days ago, Sarah became worse than I've ever seen. Not only did she scream, but she threw herself on the floor and banged her legs and body against the floor in an uncontrollable fashion. I'd never seen this behavior before, and I didn't know what to do. It was like she was possessed. I know we designed a behavioral plan for screaming, but what was I supposed to do when Sarah began throwing a tantrum and hurting herself like that? I assumed your plan possibly didn't take into account "demonic" activity. So my husband and I decided that we would just stop the time-outs. This seemed to work as she got reassured and settled down for a while (we had rid her of the demon). However, we're still at the point where tantrums and screaming are occurring on a daily basis, and we want to know what else we can do.

This scenario illustrates how a child's behavior often gets worse before it gets better. It also illustrates what parents might do when things get worse if they are not prepared ahead of time. The phenomenon of problem behavior increasing for a short time after the implementation of a behavioral plan is called an *extinction burst*. This is a short-term phenomenon (relatively speaking), but it is crucial that parents not interrupt or halt implementation of the plan during this period. Parents must be instructed before implementation on the possibility of an extinction burst and the ramifications of such. The clinician should expect that making time-outs contingent on Sarah's tantrums will initially result in all kinds of additional inappropriate behaviors, particularly when the parents attempt to impose the time-out. Sarah may scream, holler, throw herself to the floor, and attempt to run away. The parents should not be taken aback by such behaviors but must realize why they are occurring—they are intended to effect an escape from time-out—and continue forth with the planned time-out. A little education about extinction burst before implementation of the plan can often help parents make it successfully through this phenomenon. It should be emphasized that the parents need to stick to their guns in regard to the planned contingency for the problem behavior, even in the face of "demonic possessions."

The clinician might teach parents to handle the extinction burst in the manner that follows:

Clinician: I can understand how difficult it must have been to continue implementing time-outs when you saw Sarah become even more extreme in her tantrums. I'm sure it seemed like she'd lost control, but I can assure you that she was not possessed. As we discussed before implementing the time-out program, she may react to time-outs with the worst tantrum she has ever had. We need to expect that. But what we need to avoid doing is something that she expects and wants you to do: let her off the hook.

Parent: It's easy to say, but difficult to do.

Clinician: Yes, this is the toughest part—implementing the plan in the face of exacerbated behavior, which we'll call the "behavior burst" [*better term to use with parent instead of extinction burst*]. Many times things get worse before they get better. Remember, stick to your guns in the face of adversity of the kind Sarah presented. What we need to figure out is how you can support each other as you implement the time-out plan and Sarah resists. Possibly, we should initially implement the plan only at times when both of you are home, so that if one of you feels like giving in and letting Sarah out of time-out before it's over, the other one can step in and take over. Once it seems to be working, you could then go solo. Does it sound like that might help you implement time-out? Can we give it another shot?"

Parent: (*turning toward spouse*): Well, it's up to you honey. What do you think?

☐ Suggestion 5: Implementing a Child Behavior Management Plan Is Not a Part-Time Responsibility

Although it is unfortunate, implementing behavioral plans, especially in the beginning of an intervention, usually requires the increased vigilance of the parents to attend to their child's behavior. In some cases, parents can seem oblivious to aggressive or disruptive behavior occurring 3 feet away. In other cases, parents take on numerous other tasks and activities that compete with their ability to carry out the behavioral plan. Many interventions have failed because parents do not fully understand the commitment and vigilance needed to effect the plan and to make possible the change in their child's behavior. In some cases, there are early warning signs.

Clinician: Okay, Mr. and Mrs. X., we decided in our last session that we'll alter the way you respond to your daughter's disruptive behavior. We call this technique "the disruptive behavior barometer," and we'll implement it during the period after dinner—about 6 to 9 P.M. Whenever June is disruptive, as we've defined in previous sessions, move the barometer down one unit from its previous point. We'll start with 20 units, so on the first occurrence of disruptive behavior, you'd move the barometer down to 19. On the second, 18, and so forth. If the barometer goes below 11, she doesn't earn a late bedtime that night.

Parent: That sounds great. However, we'll probably have to delay implementing this treatment technique. This week Aunt Harriet is coming from Michigan, and the following week we're hosting an exchange student from Brazil. We can begin 2 weeks from now, but then we'll probably have to stop the following week because . . .

Clinician: Well, that sounds like a hectic schedule.

Yes, that *is* a hectic schedule and unfortunately one that will not lend itself to creating the conditions needed to change their child's behavior. One of the things that needs to be discussed in session with the parents is their commitment to the resources needed to implement a behavioral support plan. This may mean that they have to boil down all the activities and responsibilities they take on to the few critical ones during the period when the behavioral plan is in place. Values clarification may need to be part of the overall therapeutic plan. If the parents come to the conclusion that their child's behavior is in need of change, the clinician may be able to help them select and eliminate some of the responsibilities and activities that would interfere with the implementation of the behavioral plan.

If they are unwilling to give up some of their extensive commitments, they must understand that the conditions for creating behavior change are not going to exist, and they must be educated about the need for consistency and vigilance during behavioral plan implementation. They should decide, but the clinician needs to tell them that going into treatment in a half-hearted manner usually leads to ineffective implementation (and, consequently, is a waste of time and money).

This is not to say that a dire, rigid lifestyle devoid of all the frills needs to be adopted forever. As the child's behavior changes for the better, the intensity and vigilance required in the beginning of the behavioral plan are reduced. Furthermore, implementation of the plan becomes a more natural part of the parents' response pattern to their child's behavior.

☐ Suggestion 6: Focus on Increasing Appropriate Desirable Behavior Rather Than Just Decreasing Problem Behavior

In many of the subsequent chapters in this book, teaching and increasing appropriate desirable behavior are stressed as a preferred way to decrease targeted problem behavior. Too often, the only issue considered is the child's problem behavior. Consequently, the focus is on techniques or consequences to eliminate that behavior directly. This is illustrated particularly when parents insist they have tried everything. Yes, they have tried everything involving unpleasant consequences for undesirable behavior. However, what is often the case is that a behavioral plan for *desirable* behavior is nonexistent. It is the clinician's job to teach parents the *value and the power of positive reinforcement* of desirable behaviors. In addition to designing a major component of the comprehensive plan that focuses on delivering powerful reinforcement for appropriate behavior, the clinician must educate the parents about the need for positive reinforcement in the child's everyday life.

A hypothetical example can illustrate how to educate parents on the power of positive reinforcement. Loretta, does silly things in the home when her parents have visitors—that is, she shows off. Her parents believe that she does this for their attention, which may be correct. Therefore, Loretta's undesirable behaviors seem to get much of the visitors' attention. Because adult attention becomes a powerful reinforcer for children during times when people visit the home, it is imperative to design a strategy that will allow the parents to prompt desirable, appropriate child behaviors that will interest visitors and gain their attention, thereby making silly, obnoxious behavior less functional in getting attention. It is important to prompt the desirable behavior immediately. For example, the parents might immediately prompt Loretta in the following manner: "Loretta, can you show Mrs. Jones how you can play the piano after we talk with her for just a few minutes?" The parents must then make sure that they do talk for only a few minutes.

Children are looking for attention under such conditions as this, and they are going to get it one way or another. What parents can do is determine what desirable behaviors produce attention. Indecision in this area often results in silly behaviors occurring and being reinforced, which begins the cycle of consequences for the silly behavior and forgetting to promptly reinforce more desirable behaviors.

☐ Suggestion 7: Get Parental Follow-Through and Commitment to Implementation

Child behavior often does not change because of poor or nonexistent implementation of the plan in the home setting. In some cases, parents lack full understanding of the plan or of the need for consistency. Other times, the home situation seems to work against effective and consistent implementation of the plan. In either case, the clinician's work becomes more challenging as he or she attempts to uncover such variables and achieve the follow-through necessary for effective implementation.

Certain processes and strategies can help to achieve better follow-through and plan implementation. One strategy involves frequent monitoring and contact with the parents during the early phase of implementation. In working with parents who have children with developmental disabilities, behavioral specialists often make a home visit on the first day of implementation to catch any errors that occur right away. It is much easier to correct errors in implementation shortly after they have occurred than to correct them a week or two after the plan has come operational. To accomplish this intensive monitoring of progress, the clinician might schedule two or three mini-appointments during the first week or consider making a home visit. Frequent phone contact, directly or by leaving messages, should also be undertaken. Having their parents call in the data on a daily or period basis can be a substitute for some face-to-face visits. The parents should report the rate of the child's targeted behaviors and the number of times they effected the planned consequences for both desirable and targeted problem behaviors. They can also comment on any other aspects of the plan, such as instances in which they find it difficult to implement the plan, how they feel it is going, and so forth.

It is important in the beginning to reinforce the parents for their effort in plan implementation. It must be borne in mind that their effort will not bring about immediate behavior change in their child. The early days are when they need lots of support. Reassurance that they are headed in the right direction will sometimes maintain their behavior during this difficult period, when the absence of such reassurance could result in their dropping the plan.

☐ Suggestion 8: Balancing The Needs of the Behavior Management Strategy With the Needs of a Regular Family Life

In direct contrast to suggestion 7, the clinician needs to come to grips with the fact that implementation of a behavioral support plan 16 hours a day, 7 days a week, 365 days a year is not humanly possible. Every family has additional issues that need attention. Therefore, a delicate balance between suggestions 5 and 7 must be established.

Implementing a behavioral plan over a short time during the day, particularly around a problem setting or activity, is often most fruitful. In this manner, the parents need not implement a strategy across the entire day, but instead try to focus their attention and vigilance at a particular time when the behavior is most likely.

This is important for several reasons. First, it teaches the parents how to implement the plan over a short time. Second, it prevents their feeling that their whole life is taken up with implementing a behavioral support plan. Third, it allows them to become more vigilant about the child's behavior and their response for that short period. Finally, if behavioral change is produced, it becomes more likely that the parents will use the plan at other times during the day when those additional times are targeted.

Once the plan has been successfully implemented in one setting, it is easier to generalize use to other times when the problem behavior also occurs. After seeing some results, the parents are more likely to use this technique at other times. And they will appreciate the clinician's efforts to balance treatment with the reality and exigencies of family life.

☐ Summary

With these eight suggestions and tips, the clinician should be able to use a consultation model, either in conjunction with another service model or alone, when serving parents whose presenting issues are child problem behaviors. The following chapters address specific applications for problem behaviors and present advice packages for problem areas.

PART

II

SPECIFIC SOLUTIONS FOR SPECIFIC CHILD PROBLEMS

4

CHAPTER

Behavioral Momentum: An Effective Technique for Gaining Compliance in Young Children

A common problem cited by many parents is their inability to get their young child to comply with everyday requests and commands. "Please do this!" and "Don't Do that!" are cried hourly in many households (every minute in some cases!). Parents often report that their young child has to be told or reminded many times before compliance is obtained. In some cases, parents wonder whether the child has a hearing problem, but examination by an audiologist reveals the problem is "selective hearing." Why won't children listen?

Take the hypothetical case of Mr. and Mrs. J. and their 6-year-old son, Jason. On this particular day, it is raining. Despite the fact that Mrs. J. told Jason that he could not go out to the backyard without a raincoat, Jason has attempted multiple times to go outside without it.

Mrs. J. (*from kitchen area*): Jason, I told you to put on your raincoat. It's raining; do you want to get sick?

Jason (*from living room area*): I won't get sick. I'm eating my Wheaties. [*Begins to head out the door.*]

Mrs. J.: I'm warning you, put that raincoat on right now, or you'll be grounded.

49

Jason: Mom, I told you, I don't need it. I won't get sick. I promise. [*Heads outdoors.*]

Mrs. J. That boy, he never listens. Sometimes I think I would have to tie him to a chair to stop him. (*in a kidding manner*):

In this hypothetical scenario and many actual ones, parents find it hard to get their young children to comply with simple requests or instructions. If compliance is obtained at all, it often comes with multiple reminders, screaming, threatening or cajoling on the parts of both parents and child.

To determine whether a parent is having problems gaining compliance from their young child, the clinician should collect the following information:

1. What circumstances present the most problems with gaining compliance from their child?
2. What are some examples of commands, requests, or instructions that seem to result in noncompliance?
3. What is a reasonable estimate of the probability of compliance with the instruction or request? The parent can use the following categories to estimate the probability of compliance: N—almost never compliant (0% to 25% probability of compliance); S—sometimes compliant (26% to 50% probability); F—Fair compliance (51% to 75% probability); and U–usually compliant (76%–100% probability).

Table 1 provides an illustration of data collection with a hypothetical mother identifying six commands or instructions that she gives to her 6-year-old child on a daily basis. She indicates that five of the commands are almost never compiled with, and only one is complied with sometimes.

In reviewing these data, the clinician should look not only at the probability of compliance but also at the circumstances under which compliance is low in judging the severity of the child's noncompliance. If noncompliance is high or occurs in circumstances or situations in which most same-aged children respond readily, a behavioral plan should be considered. The clinician may need to judge whether the parents' expected level of child compliance is unrealistic. Possibly, the type of command given may be unrealistic given the child's age. If the clinician finds the parental expectations to be unrealistic, therapeutic efforts might focus on educating the parents on developmental stages and reasonable expectations for their children. If the child's noncompliance appears to be at problematic levels, however, the behavioral intervention proposed in this chapter could be entertained.

Table 1. Parent report of commands and instructions that are problems

Circumstance	Instruction	Probability of Compliance			
1 Coming in from outside	"Take your muddy shoes off."	Ⓝ	S	F	U
2 After eating	"Put your plate in the sink."	Ⓝ	S	F	U
3 Before walking to school (with mom)	"Get your lunchbox."	N	Ⓢ	F	U
4 Whenever	"Stop yelling."	Ⓝ	S	F	U
5 After school when he plays with toys	"Pick up your toys."	Ⓝ	S	F	U
6 When he undresses leaving the clothes wherever he happens to be	"Put your clothes on the chair."	Ⓝ	S	F	U

☐ Questions and Issues Involving Noncompliance of Young Children

The following four questions may arise when discussing a child's noncompliance with a parent. Also provided are suggested areas of discussion for each possible question.

Question 1: Isn't my child just going through the terrible 2's 3's?

Parents often ascribe problem behaviors to the child's age. For example, "He's just 4 years old. He doesn't know any better!" is a common explanation for a child's behavior (misbehavior). The implied assumption is that with age, the child will grow out of these behaviors or problems. Of course, there are developmental issues the clinician needs to address, but the contention that problem behavior is endemic to all 2-year-olds (or 3-year-olds, etc) needs to be discussed.

Higher levels of compliance do not automatically result when a child turns 3 years of age (or any age). If this were so, the need for Chapter 5 would be nonexistant (it addresses compliance problems with older children). In clinical practice, one needs to get parents to delineate the areas for which they wish they had better compliance and not rely on the passage of time to solve the problems. If the parenting strategy for dealing with compliance situations is flawed, the passage of time will not solve either the parents' skill deficit or the child's noncompliance with parental requests.

Another consideration needs to be presented to the parents. At some point, their child will come into contact with other adults who will have to deal with his or her behavior (e.g., in daycare, at preschool, at the neighbors'). At that point, a different judgment about acceptable levels of compliance might occur. If the young child will frequent different settings, compliance (or the lack thereof) can become a problem. The clinician should get the parents to consider intervention for compliance to ensure a more successful experience in other settings with different caretakers.

Question 2: Is it possible my child can't hear well?

To ensure that the child's hearing is not impaired, an audiologic evaluation may be in order. However, evidence of selective hearing usually can rule out hearing problems. That is, if the child attends when the parent asks him or her to engage in pleasurable activity but acts as though he or she cannot hear when asked to engage in chores, hearing and attending are indeed selective. If the parents report that the child seems to ignore them only at times when asked to do something he or she does not want to do, something other than hearing problems is likely to be the culprit.

Question 3: I don't want to pressure my child at such an early age. Could this pressure affect the child later in life?

First, many parents are under the impression that efforts to alter child behavior usually involve punitive techniques. As will be evident in this chapter, many techniques used to teach compliance are positive, preferable, acceptable methods of teaching and disciplining children.

Second, many parents have also been told by professionals that efforts to change behavior early in life adversely affect a child later in life (the notion that repressed dynamic forces find expression at later developmental stages). Without addressing what I believe is a fallacy in this theory (it is easy to detect that I am no fan of this unproven theory), let me say that it is usually a more serious issue not to address problem behaviors at an early age. What *does* affect children later in life—educationally, socially, vocationally, and so forth—is the failure to teach and develop compliance at an early age. Children who learn early in life to comply with and attend to adult instructions often lead different lives than children who do not. They are able to profit more from school experiences, get in trouble less often, and probably are better adjusted in the home. With many children, attempts to teach compliance help them lead more fulfilling lives.

Question 4: I have a big problem with tantrum behavior. How would this program address this?

Many times, a child's tantrums can be traced back to a compliance situation. For example, a child is told by his mother to put away his toys and come to the dinner table. When he does not respond (noncompliance), the mother increases the intensity of the demand and moves close to him. As the child realizes that he may be picked up and dragged over to the dinner table or the toys may taken from him, he throws a tantrum. The context for the tantrum was a compliance situation.

By addressing a child's compliance and increasing compliance to an acceptable level, tantrums usually diminish. In this example, reinforcing the child's compliance with the command to put away the toys (with praise and a tangible reinforcer) will generate future child compliance to commands and obviate the child's need for a tantrum (since he would object less to the request). Therefore, building a child's compliance with parental requests and rules often has a positive effect on other behaviors as well.

Of course, not all tantrums occur in response to parental compliance situations. In those cases, Chapter 7 (about the effective use of time-out) is relevant.

☐ Brief Description

Behavioral momentum is a technique that does what its name implies: it builds a momentum of compliance before presenting a command that is less likely to be followed. In building this momentum, the easy commands are given in rapid fashion and are met with compliance. The parent issues the targeted hard command while the behavioral momentum of compliance still exists. As a result, one gets compliance with the hard command.

☐ Empirical Basis for Behavioral Momentum Technique

Noncompliance is a common problem for parents. They often deal with severe noncompliance by "physically guiding" (i.e., dragging) their child to the area and forcing him or her to comply with the instruction. This obviously is not a preferable method, but unfortunately it is one that is frequently used. Its use is even more widespread with caregivers of persons with disabilities. However, necessity becomes the mother of invention.

Researchers at Lehigh University in Pennsylvania were interested in developing a better method for dealing with severe forms of noncompliance, one that was not dependent on the therapist's or teacher's ability to physically move the client (Mace et al., 1988). In designing a new technique, they wanted to facilitate compliance by focusing on what the caregiver does before issuing a command, rather than relying solely on the consequence for noncompliance.

In the first experiment, the researchers worked with a staff who cared for a 36-year-old man named Bart who was severely mentally retarded. He had resided in a large state-operated institution for most of his life and had a long history of not complying with staff requests. They targeted his compliance to both "do" and "don't" commands. *Do* commands were staff commands that were met with little or no compliance from Bart. They involved the performance of a simple task, for example, "Put away your lunchbox." *Don't* commands involved the discontinuation of an undesirable behavior or condition, such as "Don't leave your lunchbox on the table." The researchers identified the *do* and *don't* commands that Bart frequently did not comply with or that would in some cases make him extremely upset. These were designated "hard" commands, commands with which Bart had much difficulty complying, as verified with observational data.

Once these hard commands were identified, the researchers sought to identify "easy" commands. Easy commands were those to which Bart would respond readily. Identified easy commands included "Give me five," "Come here," "Give me a hug," and "Show me your notebook." Data collection conducted before treatment revealed that Bart's compliance with easy commands was high.

The researchers then designed a treatment that involved presenting easy commands and readily getting Bart's compliance with those before presenting a targeted hard command. This technique required the staff to develop a momentum of compliance to the easy command sequence before giving the hard command. The staff at the institution were trained to issue at least three or four easy commands to Bart before presenting a hard command. As an example, the following might occur when Bart was asked to take his shoes off the coffee table (the hard command):

1. "Bart, give me five." (Complies with easy command.)
2. "Bart, give me a hug." (Complies with easy command.)
3. "Bart, show me your notebook." (Complies with easy command.)
4. "Bart, can you take your shoes off the coffee table?" (Complies with hard command.)

Compliance is obtained for the easy commands first. After this, the hard command is issued; with subsequent compliance.

The results of this study demonstrated the efficacy of the technique of behavioral momentum. Particularly impressive was the greater effectiveness of this technique over psychotropic intervention (Haldol) for Bart's aggressive behavior. These researchers found similarly effective results with other clients in this large-scale study.

Before presenting the components of the behavioral momentum strategy, a qualification is in order. The study cited here was done with persons with developmental and learning disabilities. One might wonder whether such a technique is applicable for young children who are not disabled.

There are three points to be made in favor of using behavioral momentum with young children. First, I have successfully used this technique in clinical practice with children of preschool and kindergarten age. I therefore recommend consideration of this technique for children up to 6 or 7 years of age. If necessary, this technique can be used in conjunction with the noncompliance barometer technique described in Chapter 5.

Second, many of the behavioral techniques used today with all children were initially developed and validated in the 1960s with disabled children and adults. Behavioral momentum is a relatively recent development, and it will receive great research attention with the nonhandicapped population in the near future.

Finally, some behavioral techniques should be in the child management repertoire of all parents and future parents, and even those who do not experience severe compliance problems, and behavioral momentum is one of these. If parents learn to use behavioral momentum systematically when their children are very young, it may help prevent development of severe noncompliance problems as the children get older.

☐ Components of Behavioral Momentum

The components of the behavioral momentum strategy are the following:

1. Identify hard commands from baseline information.
2. Identify easy commands using baseline measurement procedures.

3. Present clear, unambiguous commands.
4. Identify targeted commands.
5. Design a relationship between the presentation of easy commands and the presentation of a hard command (behavioral momentum technique).
6. Reinforce compliance with easy command sequence (in isolation) periodically.

Component 1: Identifying Hard Commands

Interview data can be used to identify targeted hard commands or instructions for the child in a number of situations. Using the format detailed in Table 1, the parents could identify the commands or instructions that are either almost or never complied with or sometimes complied with to begin intervention. Once interview data on hard commands have been collected, it is wise to verify this information. The clinician should ask the parents to record the occurrence of compliance with these identified hard commands or instructions for a 1 or 2 weeks. A data sheet similar to the example provided in Table 2 can be used for this purpose.

The hypothetical data in Table 2 show three compliance episodes. Josh F., a 5-year-old boy, was asked to comply with the instructions and "Pick up your toys" (two episodes) and "Put away your coloring book." Multiple commands were given in each circumstance; that is, compliance did not occur after the first command, and his mother reissued the same request several minutes later. In the first compliance episode, recorded on Monday afternoon, Mrs. F. eventually had to drag Josh over to the toys. In the second episode, she got him to pick up his toys by "bribing" him with pudding (the incentive was given contingent on noncompliance occurring initially and was not systematically used). In the last request, "Put away your coloring book," Josh's mother never got him to put it away and eventually did it for him. One begins to see both that compliance is a problem and why it is a problem. Josh might be saying to himself, "Don't move, and the chances are 2 in 3 that she'll either do it for me or I'll get pudding if I do it!" It is hard to see why noncompliance with parental requests to put away toys or books becomes a problem.

Table 3 presents summary data on a number of hard commands that are presented around certain contexts for the hypothetical child, Josh. The parents can summarize their data in this fashion to allow for a more ready examination of the data on the clinician's part. Compliance with all requests identified in Table 3 is less than 50% during a 2-week baseline period. Matching these data with the parent interview data yields a number of targeted hard commands.

TABLE 2.   Noncompliance data sheet (1 day's worth of data)

Date: 3/26
Child: Josh F.
Age: 5

Command or Request	Time Given	Compliance
"Pick up your toys."	3:15 P.M.	No
	3:17	No
	3:23	No
	3:30	No
	3:50	No
	4:06	Yes (after yelling at him and dragging him over to the toys).
"Pick up your toys."	6:20 P.M.	No (after dinner)
	6:25	No
	6:36	No
	6:51	Yes (bribed him with pudding)
"Put away your coloring book."	7:30 P.M.	No (getting ready for bed)
	7:35	
	7:37	No
	7:38	No
	7:39	No
	7:40	No
		No (Did it for him)

Component 2: Identifying Easy Commands

In addition to collecting data on commands that parents report difficulty with, the clinician also identify what commands, requests, or verbal statements are likely to be met with compliance (i.e., easy commands). Easy commands should involve simple behaviors that take only 1 or 2 seconds to perform. They need not be commands that are essential in everyday life. Examples include "Give me a hug," "Show me your shoes," "Touch your nose," and "clap your hands." In consultation with the parents, other easy commands might also be identified. A few commands that are simple to comply with and age appropriate should be selected.

Before proceeding, it should be verified that the identified easy commands would usually result in compliance. A test condition can provide this confirmation. The parent is instructed to perform the following homework assignment. At different times, when the child is nearby, the

TABLE 3.   Compliance with hard commands across a 4-day baseline period

	Week 1	Week 2
Commands about putting away toys or material objects		
1. "Put away your toys."	20%	25%
2. "Put your dirty dishes in the sink."	40%	10%
3. "Put your pajamas in the hamper."	25%	35%
Commands around bedtime		
1. "Brush your teeth."	29%	29%
2. "Put your pajamas on."	43%	29%

parent presents one of the identified easy instructions and records whether the child complied. The parent presents each command at least five times for a 1- or 2-week period. Parents should not give more than two commands during the same compliance episode. When the parents bring these data to the clinician, they are reviewed and several easy commands or instructions are identified. Table 4 presents a hypothetical data sheet for the compliance test.

In this example, the parent collected the data on these five commands during a 2-week period. Each time the parent gave one of these five commands (e.g., "Give me a hug"), he identified the date and then circled the C if the child complied with the command at that time or the NC if the child did not comply. The percentage of compliance was then computed for each command. Based on the information presented in Table 4, all the commands except "Look at my nose" could be used as easy commands for this child.

Component 3: Presenting Clear, Unambiguous Commands

In some cases, it is unclear or ambiguous as to whether a command or request was issued or what specific behavior was being requested. The following parental statement illustrates this ambiguity: "Mommy would really like it if you would decide to get Barney and Baby Bop [stuffed animals] out of the microwave." In this example, a child was asked to make a decision. Suppose she decides that she did not want to get the stuffed animals out of the microwave. She was given that choice. It would have been much clearer if the following had been stated: "Please take Barney and Baby Bop out of the microwave before I count to 5." This

TABLE 4. Data sheet for compliance test

Command	Date	Compliance or Noncompliance	
1. "Give me a hug."	12/3	(C)	NC
	12/3	(C)	NC
	12/3	(C)	NC
	12/5	(C)	NC
	12/7	(C)	NC
2. "Touch your belly button.	12/4	(C)	NC
	12/4	(C)	NC
	12/5	(C)	NC
	12/5	(C)	NC
	12/7	(C)	NC
3. "Clap your hands."	12/4	(C)	NC
	12/5	(C)	NC
	12/7	(C)	NC
	12/7	(C)	NC
	12/8	(C)	NC
4. "Look at my nose."	12/5	(C)	NC
	12/6	C	(NC)
	12/6	C	(NC)
	12/7	(C)	NC
	12/7	C	(NC)
5. "Shake my hand."	12/3	(C)	NC
	12/4	(C)	NC
	12/4	(C)	NC
	12/5	(C)	NC
	12/6	(C)	NC

statement is clear in its intent: it is a command. A major component of any parent's repertoire in dealing with compliance situations is presenting clear, concise commands. The specific behavior or performance being requested and time limit for compliance (e.g., taking stuffed animals out of microwave by the count of 5) are precisely spelled out. The following are additional examples of clear commands and requests:

1. "Turn off the TV."
2. "Comb your hair."
3. "Please complete your math homework before 4:30 in order to watch cartoons at that time."
4. "Please pick up all the clothes in your room. Place them in the dirty clothes hamper or dresser or hang them up in the closet.

TABLE 5. Vague versus clear commands

Command (if possible, verbatim)	Vague	Clear
1. "Please hand me that toy in your hand."	V	Ⓒ
2. "Behave or else."	Ⓥ	C
3. "Turn off the TV."	V	Ⓒ
4. "Stop acting goofy."	Ⓥ	C

It would be wise for the clinician to determine whether the parents provide clear or vague commands. The parents can audiotape their interactions at times when they report child compliance is low. If the clinician reviews the audiotape and finds that the commands are ambiguous, he or she should work with the parents to teach them to present commands that specify an exact behavior or performance and the time in which it is to occur. Examples from audiotapes provide excellent relevant material.

Table 5 can be useful in determining whether the commands or instructions given during an audiotaped interview between parents and child are clear or vague. The clinician in the example wrote down verbatim the command she heard on the audiotape and whether she considered it vague or clear. This can then be used to provide feedback to the parents.

Component 4: Identifying Targeted Commands

From the list of hard commands identified previously (see Table 3), and with parental input, hard commands to be addressed immediately are identified. No more than three of four hard commands should be targeted initially. Once these initial hard commands are selected for intervention and treated effectively, additional hard commands can be selected. Table 6 illustrates the selection of initial hard commands for intervention.

Component 5: Designating the Relationship Between Easy and Hard Commands

The next step is to design the easy command sequence to be conducted before presentation of the hard command. This sequence consists of the delivery of several easy commands in rapid sequence for which compliance should readily occur. As the momentum of child compliance is built, the parent will immediately present the targeted hard command.

The behavioral momentum technique would be applied in the following manner with Josh F. When Josh's mother wants to get him to put

---

TABLE 6. Targeted hard commands

Child: Josh F.
Age: 5

1. "Pick up your toys." (with no more than four toys to be picked up initially)
2. "Put away your coloring book."
3. "Put your pajamas on."
4. "Come inside the house."

---

away his toys (hard command), she initially targets his putting away only three or four toys (a task within his current repertoire), as opposed to all toys, to promote success. The following identifies the target hard command and the easy command sequence for Josh F:

Targeted Hard Command

1. "Put away the toys in the toy box." Baseline level of compliant behavior (20% to 25%)

Easy Command Sequence (in order)

1. "Give me a hug."
2. "Touch your belly button."
3. "Clap your hands."
4. "Bend down and touch the floor." (Near the toy)

Mrs. F. wants to have Josh put away three or four of his toys in the toy box. The baseline probability of his complying with this request is between 20% and 25%. She initiates the easy command sequence before presenting the targeted hard command. She asks him to give her a hug (Josh complies), asks him to touch his belly button (he complies), quickly asks him to clap his hands (he complies), and then asks him to bend down and touch the floor. On achieving compliance with this sequence, while Josh is bent down near several toys, she presents the hard command: "Put away these toys in the toy box" (points to one or two toys). She will stay close to him, praising his initial compliance. When Josh puts away a few toys, Mrs. F. praises him, "Oh, you're such a great son!. Thank you for helping me." She then asks him if he wants to go outside and play because he was so helpful.

In implementing behavioral momentum, the following points are important:

1. The parent should be physically close to the child before issuing the first easy command.

TABLE 7. Clinicians record of five commands

Command	Within Arm's Reach	Not Within Arm's Reach
1. "Pick up your sneakers."	X	
2. "Put on a shirt."		X
3. "Don't throw the ball."	X	
4. "Sit down."		X
5. "Come here."		X

2. The easy command sequence, as well as the following hard command, should be given in rapid succession.
3. Praise should be given after each complaint behavior in the easy command sequence and also during the child's compliance with the hard command (i.e., keeps compliance going).
4. After compliance with the hard command is gained, effusive praise and a preferred activity should follow.

Before delivering the first easy command, a parent should be no more than one arm's length from the young child and facing him or her. The days of yelling the command from across the living room or kitchen are gone. This is an important requisite in the behavioral momentum technique. The clinician should provide the parent with practice, through role playing and, if possible, with their own child in the clinic. One to 2 weeks of practice in the home before intervention is also helpful.

Table 7 illustrates a clinician's record of the five commands a parent gave during a practice session in the clinic. The distance the parent was from the child when the command was given was judged by the clinician as being within arm's length or not.

The parent in Table 7 presented only two of the five commands while he was within arm's reach of the child, meaning three of the commands were given at a distance farther than an arm's length. He needs to work on this assignment at home again the following week, trying to reach the goal of all of five commands delivered within arm's reach.

A second consideration is to present the commands in rapid sequence. This means that the parent must briefly praise compliance with the easy commands and then present the next command within a few seconds. Nothing can be allowed to distract the parent or the child during the easy sequence.

When compliance occurs, the child must be praised for the effort. In the easy command sequence, the praise needs to be enthusiastic but short so that the next command can quickly follow. Also, on initial compliance with the hard command, particularly if it is a longer task or chore, the child should be praised steadily. In the previous example, when Josh was asked to put away his toys, his father praised him as soon as he put his hands on the first toy. Compliance with the hard command may require steady praise while the child is performing the task so that momentum is not lost.

A final related consideration is to reinforce compliance with the hard command. The behavioral momentum treatment strategy described here works initially as a way to "slide in" a targeted hard command in the presence of compliance with easy commands. One must realize, however, that noncompliance is often due to the lack of reinforcement for compliance. It is therefore imperative that the parents be taught to follow compliance with the hard command with praise and two additional conditions: a preferred activity and absence of another command for a period of time (e.g., 10 to 15 minutes).

The following scenario illustrates what can go wrong when a child's compliance with hard commands is followed by the issuance of another command:

Wrong

Johnny has been working on his coloring book, and he puts it down next to the crayons to go to the bathroom. Since it is time for him to get ready for bed (and his mother always reads a story to him at that time), she wants him to put his crayons and book away before getting into bed. She goes over to him before issuing any command, makes eye contact with him, and then says, "Can you show me which crayon is purple?" Johnny smiles and points to the purple crayon. Then she asks, "Can you put the purple crayon here in the box next to the blue one?" Johnny complies. She uses this nifty strategy until all the crayons are back in the box an then asks Johnny to put the crayons and coloring book on his desk, which he does. She says to herself, "Boy, have I got him on a *roll*! This stuff really works! I'll have him clean up the toys in the living rom before he goes to bed." Johnny comes back, getting ready for his story when she says, "Johnny, go into the living room and pick up your toys and put them in the toy box." Johnny whines, cries, and refuses to do this. She had him and then she lost him.

The next scenario shows the correct way to implement behavioral momentum in the context of reinforcing compliance with the hard command:

Right

Johnny has been working on his coloring book, and he puts it down next to the crayons to go to the bathroom. Since it is time for him to get ready for bed (and his mother always reads a story to him at that time), she wants him to put his crayons and book away before getting into bed. She goes over to him before issuing any commands, makes eye contact with him, and then says, "Can you show me which crayon is purple?" Johnny complies. She uses this nifty strategy until all the crayons are back in the box and then asks Johnny to put the crayons and coloring book on his desk, which he does. Once Johnny puts his coloring book and crayons on the desk, his mother says, "Oh, thank you so much! You're such a big help!" She gives him a hug. "How about you pick out your favorite story tonight!" She knew when to declare Johnny's efforts a success. Next week she can work on getting the toys picked up. Way to go, Mom!

To illustrate behavioral momentum in operation, the following two scenarios demonstrate a mother/child compliance interaction. In the first, the parent does not use behavioral momentum. In the second, she does.

Absence of Behavioral Momentum

Rhianna is throwing the ball against the side of the house, which makes her mother nervous as the ball gets close to the window. Her mother requests, "Rhianna, don't throw the ball against the side of the house; it might hit the window." Rhianna continues to throw the ball against the side of the house, even in the face of stronger verbal statements by her mother to desist from such action. Finally, it hits the window. At that point, her mother rushes out and grabs the ball out of her hand, scolds her, and tells her to go to her room, causing Rhianna to have a tantrum and run around the yard.

Using Behavioral Momentum

Rhianna is again throwing the ball against the side of the house. Her mother comes outside and issues three easy commands, starting with "Rhianna, can I get a hug from you?" Rhianna drops the ball and gives her mom a hug. Her mother then asks her, "Rhianna, can you throw me the ball?" Rhianna says, "Sure, mom," and complies with the request. Her mother then requests, "Rhianna, can you throw the ball against this fence for me?" Rhianna complies. Then, "Rhianna, can you not throw the ball against the side of the house for the next 10 minutes until I can come out here to play with you?" She responds, "Yes." Case solved!

TABLE 8.   Schedule for embedding easy Commands in daily activities

Date	Activity	Number of Embedded Easy Commands
4/21–4/30	Morning—breakfast	3–5
	Afternoon—storytime	4–9
	Evening—before bedtime	2–5

Component 6: Reinforcement of Compliance With Easy Commands in Isolation Periodically

The parents should be taught to deliver easy command sequences periodically at times when child compliance with a hard command is not needed. Further, they should reinforce compliance at these times with attention, praise, and some tangible reinforcers. This is extremely important and cannot be overstated. If the easy commands are given only when a hard command is imminent, the child will discern this and stop responding to the easy command sequence. The child will associate the parent's presence and the presentation of specific easy commands with an impending hard command. It is important to make sure that the issuance of the easy command sequence does not set the stage for the deliverance of a hard command all the time. Sometimes the parents can just let the child show off to the easy commands!

The clinician should set a schedule for the parent to issue easy commands each day. They might agree to present the easy command sequence twice each day (in isolation). Table 8 illustrates a schedule for the parents that designates the times during the day when the easy commands will be given (in isolation) and reinforced. The easy commands are embedded in naturally occurring activities. Of course, you want to periodicaly change the activity that the easy command sequence is embedded in so that a generalized response to these commands occurs irrespective of the time they are given.

☐ Questions Concerning Behavioral Momentum Technique

Following are some questions parents may have about behavioral momentum. Clinicians can use the responses detailed here as suggestions to guide their explanations to parents, should these or similar questions arise.

Question 1: How many hard commands should be targeted?

For noncompliant children, there will be a host of identified hard commands. It is wise to initially target a small number of hard commands if the child demonstrates widespread noncompliance. If other techniques are being used in conjunction with behavioral momentum, it might be feasible to target more instructions. Once success is achieved with the three or four initially targeted commands, other commands can be targeted.

Question 2: What if the child does not comply with the hard command?

If compliance with the hard command is not obtained, the parents should be taught to initiate the easy command sequence again to regain a momentum of compliance. This time, when the hard command sequence is delivered, the parents should make sure that the child complies by giving as much help as needed for the child to "get it going." Of course, praise and other reinforcement should follow compliance.

Question 3: What if the child does not respond to the easy command sequence?

If the child does not comply with the easy command sequence, it is important not to issue the hard command. The clinician must teach the parents that when this happens, they do not have a momentum of compliance but rather may be generating a momentum of noncompliance. In this circumstance, the parents should go back to the easy command sequence that obtained compliance earlier. When a momentum of compliance is gained, the hard command sequence can be tried again. Behavioral momentum is effective only when the parents can generate a momentum of compliance.

The following example illustrates the sequence of easy commands given by the parent and subsequent compliance (or lack thereof): "Johnny, touch my nose! (child complies). "Johnny, tell me your house address" (he verbally complies). "Johnny, please stand up" (he does not comply). On noncompliance with the command to standup, the parent would repeat the previously presented easy commands before reissuing the command to stand.

If the parent is using a designated easy command sequence, it is reasonable to expect that compliance occur most of the time. If noncompliance is occurring more frequently with one of the easy commands in the sequence, it is possible that this is not an easy command. This can be verified by watching the child or presenting the easy command sequence during therapy. If a command is not generating a high level of compliance, it should be pulled out of the sequence and designated a hard command (and possibly be targeted for compliance using behavioral momentum).

Question 4: What are some ways behavioral momentum can be rendered ineffective?

The following conditions can render behavioral momentum ineffective: (1) failure to use the easy command sequence before presenting the hard command, (2) failure to build a momentum of compliance to the easy commands before issuing the hard commands, (3) failure to praise compliance with the easy command sequence, and (4) failure to reinforce compliance with a targeted hard command with a preferred activity.

The behavioral momentum technique works on the basis of a series of easy commands that generate compliance. Sometimes the parents may forget and deliver the targeted hard command abruptly. This, of course, does not build the compliance momentum needed. The parent must understand that the easy command sequence should always be presented before the hard command is given (until it becomes an easy command).

If noncompliance occurs within the easy command sequence, noncompliance with the following hard command would also be probable. Again, the clinician must make sure the parents understand that they need to generate a momentum of compliance to obtain compliance with the targeted hard command.

It is also essential that parents praise compliance with the easy command sequence. The failure to give reinforcement to the child for complying with targeted command by providing a highly preferred event is another way in which behavioral momentum can be rendered ineffective. If compliance with a command is always followed by the presentation of a less desirable activity or event, the child will begin to not comply because he or she knows that something undesirable is forthcoming. The parents should try to provide a desirable activity if *compliance* occurs, particularly with younger children (some people call this redirecting the child's attention). With older children, one can use the noncompliance barometer (see Chapter 5) to provide a conditional incentive for compliance with parental commands.

Question 5: What if behavioral momentum is ineffective?

In some cases, behavioral momentum is not effective in getting young children to comply, particularly when a parent wants the child to stop or desist a pleasurable activity. In some cases, a time-out consequence can be an additional effective strategy in reducing noncompliance.

When using time-out as an addition to behavioral momentum, the clinician should teach the parent the following guidelines:

1. Specify (a priori) the length of the time-out.
2. To make sure the time-out occurs immediately after the noncompliance (e.g., verbal refusal) and occurs consistently.
3. To a select a few targeted hard commands to use with time-out.
4. Go back and present the targeted command that was in effect subsequent to the time-out (see Chapter 7 for greater details on using time-out).

The following is a hypothetical example of the use of time-out as a consequence for a child's not complying with the parent's command to not pull on the window curtains.

> Mrs. S. knows that Bobby is pulling on the window curtains and moves over to him and provides the following easy commands: (1) "Bobby, look at me" (complies); (2) "Bobby, can you shake my hand?" (complies); and (3) "Bobby, give me a hug" (Bobby does not comply but instead pulls on the curtains). Because Bobby did not comply with this last request, Mrs. S. decides to use a time-out at this point. She says, "Bobby, you cannot pull on the curtains," and physically moves him to the time-out chair. She sets the timer and informs Bobby that he must remain in his seat for 3 minutes. If Bobby gets up before the 3-minute period is over, she immediately places him back in the chair, and *resets the timer* for an additional 3 minutes. After the 3-minute period is up, Mrs. S. brings Bobby back to the area around the window curtains and goes through the same sequence. "Bobby, please look at me" (complies), "Bobby, shake my hand" (complies), "Bobby, give me a hug" (complies), and "Bobby, don't pull on the curtains" (complies). She then gives him an alternate activity. "Bobby, come over here and play with your Mighty Morphin Power Rangers. I'll get them down for you."
>
> The time-out occurred immediately and for a prescribed period. Subsequent to that time-out, Mrs. S. re-created the scenario in which the noncompliance occurred by repeating the easy sequence followed by the hard command. Also, contingent on compliance to the *don't* command, Mrs. S. provided Bobby with a highly preferred activity.

The following important steps in implementing time-out in this example should be noted:

1. It occurred immediately after the noncompliance with an easy command, which was coupled with Bobby's continuing to pull on the curtains.
2. Bobby was physically taken to time-out, avoiding the verbal argument that often ensues when a parent wants the child to go under his or her own direction
3. A timer was set for 3 minutes, designating the length of time Bobby was to remain in time-out.
4. If Bobby had gotten up before 3 minutes, he would have immediately been placed back into time-out and the timer reset for 3 minutes.
5. The compliance sequence was repeated after Bobby did a continuous 3-minute time-out. If noncompliance occurs, the time-out procedure is immediately initiated again.
6. Contingent on compliance, reinforcement is delivered.

A second technique to use in addition to the behavioral momentum technique is the compliance barometer. This technique is described in greater detail in Chapter 5. In brief, the technique requires the parent to engage in several behaviors when noncompliance occurs. Each time the child does not comply with a parental command, the noncompliance barometer is moved down one level. If the barometer stays above a certain standard, the child earns a special reinforcer or highly preferred event. If the child is capable of understanding this, the parents and clinician can consider using this technique in conjunction with behavioral momentum and time-out as techniques to treat noncompliance (when behavioral momentum alone is ineffective).

☐ Summary

Noncompliance in young children is not an inherent circumstance parents have to endure until the child gets older. Using behavioral momentum, parents can teach young children the value of following instructions and requests. By presenting easy commands and building a momentum of compliance, the parent is able to slide in a hard command and gain compliance. Most importantly, the parent praises compliance and reinforces it by allowing the child to engage in a desirable preferred activity. Compliance will become a likely event only if the consequences for such behavior are usually desirable.

When noncompliance is not treated in young children, it often persists into their later years, when it can become more of a problem. Chapter 5 addresses noncompliance in older children and adolescents.

The Noncompliance Barometer and Compliance in Older Children

Chapter 4 presented the behavioral momentum technique for parents to use with younger children when issues of compliance arise. This chapter presents a technique applicable for children of elementary school age and older. With older children, one can rely to a greater degree on powerful positive consequences for a child's compliance with parental instructions or task demands. With them, incentives for compliance can play a more influential role. This is not to say that behavioral momentum would not be a good strategy to use on occasion with older children to obtain initial compliance to a few targeted parental commands. However, its exclusive use may not be effective over the long term. This chapter presents a technique that allows parents to encourage a child's compliant behavior throughout the day by setting up an undesirable consequence for non-compliance each time it occurs.

The same assessment information delineated in Chapter 4 would be applicable here as well. In addition to inquiry about commands or requests that seem to generate high levels of child noncompliance, the clinician can also inquire about tasks or chores that often result in non-compliance (using the same format as delineated in Table 2 of Chapter 4). The same issues presented in Chapter 4 on determining the extent and severity of noncompliance in young children are applicable here as well.

10
9
8
7
6
5
4
3
2
1

FIGURE 1.   Noncompliance barometer showing full 10 units.

☐   Brief Description

The technique I call the *noncompliance barometer* uses a fine system to decrease noncompliant behavior in children. The noncompliance barometer is simple in design and implementation. It allows parents to monitor and reinforce compliance across long periods of time, without delivering primary reinforcers at each occurrence. The noncompliance barometer requires the parent to present the child with a stipend or number of points at the beginning of the time period. When noncompliant behavior occurs, a point or stipend amount is taken or removed—that is, a fine is imposed. If, at the end of the period, the stipend amount or point amount is above a designated level, the child earns a reinforcer selected by him or her.

A noncompliance barometer is illustrated in Figure 1. The child starts with a value of 10. This could be 10 points or 10 units of money (e.g., 10 nickels, 10 quarters). The 10 units are clear initially to indicate that the child currently has all units. Each time the targeted noncompliance behavior occurs, one unit is shaded to indicate loss of that unit. Figure 2 illustrates the barometer's being moved down one unit as a result of the occurrence of a targeted behavior. A line drawn across the barometer indicates the unit point at which the child loses access to the primary reinforcer. By the end of the time period, if the barometer has dropped below the line, the reinforcer is lost. If the barometer stays above the line, the child earns the privilege or reinforcer.

The noncompliance barometer can also use a monetary stipend system, in which the child starts with an amount (e.g., $1.00) for the day or

10
9
8
7
6
5
4
3
2
1

FIGURE 2. Noncompliance barometer showing loss of one unit (shaded). Line between 5 and 6 indicates acceptable criterion.

period. When a fine is levied for an act of noncompliance, the barometer moves down one unit, representing the amount of the fine. In Figure 3, a noncompliance barometer begins with a $1.00 stipend, and fine amounts of 10¢ each are marked. Therefore, the maximum number of fines for the designated period would be 10, at which point the child would have lost the entire stipend.

☐ Empirical Basis for the Noncompliance Barometer

Common child problem behaviors in elementary school settings often include off-task and rule violations. These behaviors occur not only in children with severe behavior problems but also in average to good students on occasion. A technique that provides incentives for other appropriate behaviors and that removes incentives when problem behaviors occur would benefit many children (as well as the teachers).

A study conducted in a special education class on a regular elementary school campus in Tallahassee, Florida, sought to determine whether a response-cost system could decrease a reported high degree of off-task and disruptive behavior (Iwata & Bailey, 1974). The mean age of the students in the class was 10 years, and the mean IQ was 70. The study took place during the math period when students were given math problems to complete.

The two categories of student behavior that were the targets of the study were off-task behavior and rule violations. Off-task behavior was

$1.00
.90
.80
.70
.60
.50
.40
.30
.20
.10

FIGURE 3.   Noncompliance barometer showing a monetary system.

defined as a child's visual nonattention to the instructional materials for more than 2 seconds, unless the student was either talking to the teacher or had his or her hand raised above the head. Rule violations were behaviors that violated one or more of the teacher-prepared rules. The teacher's rules involved remaining seated, raising one's hand to get help, not talking or disturbing other students, and taking turns using the bathroom.

The technique the researchers used to decrease rule violations was the following: Every student in one of the experimental groups received a cup containing 10 tokens. They could keep all 10 tokens given to them if they followed the rules. However, they would lose tokens for breaking rules. With each rule violation, 1 token was taken; this was called a response-cost or fine. The students were told that they had to have at least 6 tokens in their cup at the end of the math period to earn a snack. The children earned a snack contingent on their behavior (see illustration of fine system presented in Table 1). On the sixth day of the intervention, the criterion for snacks was raised to 8 tokens.

The plan also provided an additional component, called student "surprise days." Three or four students who had earned the most tokens since the last surprise day were eligible for a special bonus. Since the surprise days were not announced ahead of time, the students were told it was

TABLE 1.   Basic Contingencies of Study

Rule violation occurred→	Loss of token
Loss of more than 4 tokens→	Loss of snack at end of math period

important for them to accumulate as many tokens as possible to become eligible for the surprise day bonus.

The fine strategy decreased rule violations dramatically. In addition, off-task behavior, which did not result in the removal of a token, also decreased to low levels, often below 10% (baseline rates hovered and exceeded 35% to 40%).

Although this study dealt with rule violations in school, the nature of the treatment can be applied to noncompliance problems if the following two conditions are met. First, the child has an understanding of quantity. Second, the child needs minimal physical guidance or help to perform the requested task or behavior.

☐ Components of the Noncompliance Barometer Program

To implement the noncompliance barometer program for child noncompliance, the following components are needed:

1. Definition of child noncompliance for the targeted times or situations
2. Collection of baseline data
3. Definition of the fine contingency
4. Selection of the initial standard for reinforcement
5. Identification of the reinforcer to be delivered
6. Parental training in program implementation
7. Progressive alteration of the standard over time

Component 1: Definition of Noncompliance

The definition of noncompliance usually requires two factors: (1) specification of what constitutes an act of compliance, thereby defining the absence of such an act as noncompliance, and (2) specification of a length of time to initiate movement or to complete the desired task or behavior. The first factor is the easiest to specify. Noncompliance is defined as the absence of compliant behavior. For example, if the child was asked to make the bed and the bed wasn't made, noncompliance occurred. In some cases, the clinician may need to help the parent define specifically what behavior or performance is being requested, such as what constitutes that a bed that is "made." Table 2 presents several criteria that define a bed that is made for a hypothetical 10-year-old child.

In addition to determining the behavioral criteria for noncompliance, the clinician helps determine the time limit for defining a compliant act.

TABLE 2.   Criteria detailing a bed that is made

1. Clean pillowcases
2. Lack of crease in pillowcase
3. Clean bed sheet and top sheet
4. Lack of crease in bed sheet and top sheet
5. Corners tucked in at bottom of bed
6. Top sheet folded over bed sheet by pillow

The importance of setting a time limit that defines compliance is obvious for many parents, who feel it takes forever for their children to complete tasks. For example, the father asks his daughter to put her sneakers in the closet. Five minutes later, the sneakers are not put away. He asks her why the sneakers are not in the closet. The daughter's answer is obvious: "I'm getting to it!" The father indicates to her that he meant for her to put them away in the immediate future. Unfortunately, her definition of "immediate future" and his do not match. Specifying a time period in which the child either initiates movement or completes the task removes the doubt about when the task should be completed. It therefore clarifies when an act of noncompliance occurs.

In research studies, the time period in which the child should initiate movement to be compliant is usually 3 to 5 seconds (Cipani, 1994). One simple technique for monitoring child initiation is to count (either overtly or covertly) using "one Mississippi, two Mississippi" to the designated time of 3 or 5 seconds. If the child does not initiate movement by the time the parent finishes counting, noncompliance has occurred. For example, the parent would present the following instruction, "I want you to put your sneakers in the closet right now, picking them up before I get to five!" (and then parent counts to five). If the child initiates movement to comply before five is reached, compliance has occurred.

Specifying a time limit for task completion requires more flexibility. The length of time needed to complete a task depends on the nature of the task. The amount of time designated for each task needs to be ironed out with the parents. A fairly simple, straightforward task may not require much time (e.g., putting books or a backpack on a desk.) In other cases, the task may be lengthier, such as making ones' own breakfast in the morning. The time limit that defines compliance needs to be longer for the more difficult task.

The general method of monitoring time limits of some duration is use of a kitchen timer set for the designated period. Noncompliance occurs if the task is not completed when the timer rings. Table 3 provides a schedule sheet for several common morning tasks and the length of time allotted for completion by a hypothetical parent for her 11-year-old daughter,

TABLE 3.   Parent checklist for morning tasks for Samantha

Time Allotted	Morning Tasks	Completed	
30 min	Getting ready for breakfast (bath/shower taken, groomed, dressed appropriately for weather, teeth brushed, bed made)	(Yes)	No
10 min	Making own breakfast (cereal or microwavable breakfast)	(Yes)	No
10 min	Getting ready for school (cleaning up breakfast area, backpack assembled, coat ready if needed)	(Yes)	No

Samantha. Each time Samantha completes the task within the time allotted, compliance is recorded (mother circles yes).

In the example in Table 3, Samantha is given 30 minutes to complete all the activities under associated with getting ready for breakfast. As her mother wakes Samantha at 6:25 A.M., she sets a kitchen timer for 30 minutes. When Samantha is done, she is allowed to make her breakfast (for which 10 minutes is allotted). The timer is reset. After she eats (not a compliance problem), she has to perform several other the tasks to get ready for school—clean up breakfast area, assemble backpack, and get coat or sweater if needed. Samantha will earn time to watch TV in the morning if she completes three tasks in the time allotted.

Component 2: Collection of Baseline Data

Before implementing the noncompliance barometer program, the clinician requests the parents to collect several days of baseline data. This is necessary because these data are used to set the behavioral standard needed for reinforcement. During designated time periods, the parents record each command or request given (as well as the nature of the command) and the number of times the child did not comply within the designated time limit. Table 4 provides an example of 5 days of baseline data collected on a 7-year-old child's level of noncompliance to two commands during mealtime. The number of commands given ranges between 12 and 18 and the rate of noncompliance is over 50%. The proportion and percentage of noncompliance with parental requests not to play with silverware, plates, and glasses on the dinner table and not to play with or throw food are provided for each day. These summary data provide a quick picture of what went on each day at the dinner table.

TABLE 4. Daily summary of baseline data

Type of Command	Frequency of Command	Frequency of Noncompliance	% of Noncompliance
Date: 3/21			
1. "Don't play with silverware, plates, or glasses."	15	10	67%
2. "Don't play with or throw food."	13	11	85%
Date: 3/22			
1. "Don't play with silverware, plates, or glasses."	24	16	67%
2. "Don't play with or throw food."	18	10	56%
Date: 3/23			
1. "Don't play with silverware, plates, or glasses."	17	10	59%
2. "Don't play with or throw food."	14	8	57%
Date: 3/25			
1. "Don't play with silverware, plates, or glasses."	21	13	62%
2. "Don't play with or throw food."	28	14	50%
Date: 3/27			
1. "Don't play with silverware, plates, or glasses."	22	18	82%
2. "Don't play with or throw food."	26	19	73%

Component 3: Definition of Fine Contingency

At this stage, clinician and parents define the fine component of the noncompliance barometer program. On the occurrence of a noncompliant behavior, the fine is effected. The nature of the fine contingency of the noncompliance barometer, is as follows:

Does not comply with→   barometer level
instruction or request   moved down one unit

Specific hypothetical examples of the cost-response contingency for noncompliant behaviors follow:

TABLE 5.   Rules for moving the noncompliance
Instances of Failure to Comply—Barometer Moves Down One Unit
1. Roxana fails to lower TV volume by the count of 10 when given command.
2. Roxana does not put her cup and plate away in sink after afternoon snack within 1 minute of command.
3. Roxana does not comply with simple instructions during the afternoon within 5 seconds of command.

Specific Hypothetical Application 1
    If Johnny does not make→   Barometer level
    his bed within 5 minutes of command   moved down one unit

Specific Hypothetical Application 2
    If Tamika does not pick her→   Barometer level
    clothes off of the bed and hang them   moved down one unit
    up within 1 minute of command

Specific Hypothetical Application 3
    If Robert does not come inside→   Barometer level
    for dinner within 2 minutes of moth-   moved down one unit
    er's calling him

A helpful tool for parents is a table or chart listing specific examples of noncompliance that will result in the fine contingency. Table 5 is a hypothetical example of such a chart for Roxana, an 8-year-old girl on the noncompliance barometer program. It specifies that the barometer moves down one unit if any of those three noncompliant acts occur. The first two are fairly specific, but the third is general. The third rule allows for any other instruction issued during the afternoon period to fall under the rubric of a compliance situation capable of generating a consequence. Such a chart could be posted for both parents and daughter to see.

Component 4: Selection of the Standard for Reinforcement

The selection of the initial behavioral standard for reinforcement—where the thick line is drawn on the noncompliance barometer—is based on the child's baseline level of noncompliance. The clinician and parent should attempt to select an initial behavioral standard that allows the child to easily succeed on the program. The behavioral standard becomes more

TABLE 6.   Jose's baseline level of compliance in the afternoons and evenings during school days (target times)

Date	Requests	Compliance Responses	Compliance Percentage
2/15	10	6	60%
2/16	14	7	50%
2/17	5	3	60%
2/18	11	5	45%
2/19	14	8	57%
2/21	10	3	30%
2/22	12	6	50%
Overall compliance rate = 50%			

The proportion of requests compiled with is the compliance ratio.

stringent once success is generated early in the program. Examples of the right and wrong way to select the initial criterion level are presented here, and are based on the data in Table 6.

Right Method of Criterion Selection

The clinician and Jose's parents notice that noncompliance was at or less than 50% on 4 of the 7 days baseline data were collected. They therefore selected noncompliance levels that did not exceed 50% as the initial criterion level for earning the reinforcer (30 minutes of extra TV time or Nintendo time). They set up a barometer with 10 units. If Jose stayed above units of the barometer (five noncompliant behaviors) for a set of 10 commands or instructions, he earned the reinforcer (time could be accrued throughout the day to be exchanged between 6:30 and 8:00 that evening). On the basis of this standard, the clinician and Jose's parents believed he would meet with success initially. The standard would then be increased 1 unit when Jose's barometer remained at or about 5 units eight consecutive times.

Wrong Method of Criterion Selection

After reviewing the baseline data, Jose's parents and the clinician choose to ignore it. His parents remarked, "He can do better! He just needs a kick in the pants! That'll get him moving!" Against her better judgment, the clinician agreed with Jose's parents (about the kick in the pants, too). They set the standard at 9 units or above. Jose did not achieve the behavioral standard on the first six barometers. Consequently, his parents dropped the program and took him to a neurologist to have "his head examined."

Component 5: Selection of a Reinforcer

Selecting the reinforcer that the child will earn is similar in process to other programs explained in this book. The type of reinforcer that can be earned as well as when the child can have the event or object needs to be determined before implementation. In addition, the child should also be afforded a period of time-off, when the parents do not present any additional tasks or requests—in other words, they give him or her a break.

Listed here are some sample behavioral contracts for two hypothetical children on the noncompliance barometer program:

Melinda: If Melinda stays *above 17 units* on the 25-unit noncompliance barometer, *she earns a choice of dessert that evening and a free half hour* (no tasks given during that time).

Roberto: If Roberto stays above 10 quarters on the 12-quarter noncompliance barometer for a given day, he may keep all the money that day. If he falls below 7 quarters, he keeps none of the stipend. If he is between 7 and 10 quarters he can keep half of the quarters left. (Guess where the baseline data indicated a good start point was).

Component 6: Parental Training

In addition to teaching the parents the specifics of the noncompliance barometer program, the clinician may also need to teach basic effective parenting skills for compliance situations. The following four components constitute an effective parental repertoire in compliance situations:

1. Parent is close to child before delivering the command.
2. Parent gains child's attention.
3. Parent presents clear statement about the behavior or performance expected.
4. Parent issues the request or command once.

Too often, parents issue commands or instructions when the child is too far away, not realizing that the child has a distance advantage, and is therefore less likely to comply (i.e., "She's too far away from me; She won't come and get me!") In contrast, the parental compliance repertoire package requires parents to get close (initially) to the child before delivering the command. They must also gain the child's attention (i.e., face to face contact) before issuing a command. This is done by calling his or her name or saying "Look at me," whichever is more effective.

Parents also have to be taught to be explicit in their requests and commands (see Chapter 4 for examples). It is often unclear what child behavior is being requested and whether it is a request, a choice, or simply a statement. It must be a request or a command.

Finally, parents are taught to issue the instruction only once and then to deliver consequences as a function of compliance or noncompliance. Many parents are used to repeating a request or command many times to gain compliance. They must learn to issue an instruction once and then follow through with consequences if noncompliance occurs. A practice role-play session in the clinician's office may be of help.

The following illustration of the implementation of these four components in a compliance situation in which the father wants his daughter to turn the CD player to a lower volume.

> The father moves within arm's reach of his daughter, who is next to the CD player, singing and dancing in her room (proximity), and says, "Julie, can I have your attention for a minute?" (Attention gaining.) "The music is a bit too loud for your mother and me, and I need you to turn it down to no higher than 5 right now, please." (clear statement of behavior to be performed) (The father begins counting to "five Mississippi overtly (specified time criteria for compliance). Julie lowers the volume.

In another example, a mother requests that her son clear off the dining table:

> The mother is in the kitchen area and walks over to her son, George, and gets in front of him and says, (close proximity and attention gaining), "George I need you to do something for me. I need you to clean off the dining table. Take off the dirty glasses and dishes, put them in the sink, and put the utensils in the dishwasher. Once all the dishes, glasses, and utensils have been removed from the table and placed in the sink or dishwasher area, I need you to take a cloth that is slightly wet and wipe the table off. I'll set the oven timer for 4 minutes and if all that is completed, you have finished the task and can go outside and play" (clear delineation of performance).

Component 7: Making the behavioral standard more stringent

As has been alluded to, the initial selection of the behavioral standard is based on prior baseline data. The standard is selected so that the child will succeed on the plan in the first few days of implementation. However, once he or she has earned reinforcement consistently in the early days of the program, a new standard can be selected and designated with parental input. It may be wise for the clinician to give the parents an overview of how the behavioral standard is determined so that they understand how noncompliance will gradually be reduced over time by progressively altering the standard.

The following is a hypothetical case in which the clinician explains the process to the parents of Nicole as it relates to the noncompliance barometer program.

Clinician: In reviewing the data, I see that Nicole has done extremely well. She was successful in reaching the daily goal of less than five instances of noncompliance when you and she are getting ready to go to work and school in the morning on 8 of 9 days. How do you feel about this? Are you pleased with her progress?

Parent: She sure keeps track of how far the barometer drops and has really learned to stop being oppositional, particularly when the barometer is near the line. But can't we just go for no acts of noncompliance as the goal, and Nicole gets the money only then?

Clinician: I can appreciate your need to get faster results, but let's take things a little slower. Remember, we discussed how we would shape Nicole's noncompliance to your task demands in the morning gradually, so that we won't lose the positive momentum that has been built so far. Feel good about the progress to date. You and your husband (and family if you choose) should celebrate this success. Treat yourselves to something special tonight.

What I recommend is that we change the goal to three or fewer acts of noncompliance. Given the data for the past 9 days, it looks like Nicole will be successfully at least 4 of the next 9 days, and based on what you've told me, I think she can demonstrate enough self-control to achieve this new standard. How does this sound?

Parent: Well, I'll go along with that.

Clinician: Remember its better to bet in favor of success, by selecting a standard that would be easier to achieve, than to risk program failure by selecting a standard that's too difficult. If Nicole failed to achieve the goal repeatedly, she might just give up. Then we'd have to go back to the

7
6
5
4
3
2
1
0

FIGURE 4.   Compliance barometer for evening TV.

beginning. Be proud of what's been accomplished. You're on the right track. Keep up the good work!

☐ Compliance Barometer

The noncompliance barometer requires the clinician to gather the baseline rate of noncompliance and then use a cost-response procedure to effect reinforcement for lowered levels of noncompliance. However, one could choose to reduce noncompliance by targeting compliance for an increase (obviously, as noncompliance goes down, compliance goes up). The same monitoring techniques described earlier can be used, but instead of using a fine for noncompliance from a designated point amount or stipend, points are given for compliance. In other words, the child starts at the bottom of the barometer 0 and with each act of compliance, he or she moves up one unit. This technique is called the *compliance barometer* and uses a barometer in tracking the occurrence of child compliance with parental requests or demands across a designated period or across the entire day.

A compliance barometer is depicted in Figure 4. In this example, the child begins at the bottom of the barometer (unit value 0). With each act of compliance during the designated period (e.g., during evening TV watching), the level in the barometer moves up one unit. If at the end of the TV time (e.g., 1 hour), the barometer is above the thick line—in this case 5 units or above—the child earns reinforcement (e.g., an extra half hour of TV). If the level is below the line, the child does not earn reinforcement.

The steps to implement use of the compliance barometer are similar to those designated for the noncompliance barometer. They are listed here with the necessary changes to account for targeting compliance as a behavior to increase:

1. Definition of compliance for the targeted times or situations.
2. Collection of baseline data.
3. Definition of point or monetary contingency for compliance.
4. Selection of the initial criterion for reinforcement.
5. Identification of the reinforcers to be delivered.
6. Parental training in program implementation.
7. Increase in stringency of criteria for reinforcement over time.

☐ Questions About Implementing the Noncompliance Barometer

Below are some parental questions that may arise during use of the noncompliance barometer. Suggestions for responding to them are provided.

Question 1: What if my child refuses to comply with the task or chore? Should I move down more than one level?

In some situations, parents feel the need to strengthen the fine consequence when faced with oppositional, noncompliant behavior. The tendency on the part of many parents is to double or triple the fine. This potential situation should be addressed before treatment begins.

An arbitrary decision to take more points than agreed on or to move down multiple levels on the noncompliance barometer can often have a deleterious effect on the program. Parents need to be reminded that the behavioral standard was set on the basis of obtained data. The clinician took into account the number of times noncompliance occurred and used that as the basis for selecting a reasonable starting point. If the parent decides to occasionally double (or triple) the fine, the standard may not be appropriate to obtain success.

If some acts of noncompliance are more severe, perhaps they can be defined and dealt with separately, through either increasing the fine consequences or using another technique. This should be a joint decision with the clinician included. If an additional fine is to be imposed for certain acts of noncompliance, these need to be delineated a priori. Again, this should be a joint decision.

Question 2: Is it better to use the compliance barometer or the noncompliance barometer?

In some cases, parents may want to use the compliance barometer, believing that it is better to pay attention to compliance when it occurs, rather than focus on noncompliance. If they want to use a compliance barometer, so be it. Research has found the two barometers to be equally effective. Additionally, the clinician should indicate that the use of the noncompliance barometer does not preclude the use of praise and parental attention for compliance. When a command is given and the child complies, the parent could deliver praise.

In cases in which many commands are given across a day, parents eventually find it easier to record when noncompliance occurs (as this becomes a lower frequency event). Recording frequent acts of child compliance requires much more effort and in the long run may result in more *parental* noncompliance through consistent implementation. In my clinical work, parents and teachers most often practice a fine system for providing consequences (given their other duties). But, again, either method is fine.

Question 3: My child can become rather defiant. Will this technique work for extremely oppositional children?

It is hard to answer this question on an individual basis. One never knows what will work in any given case. However, we do know that the non-compliance barometer will *not* work if it is not implemented correctly or is not implemented at all.

Perhaps the best way to answer this question is to tell the parents, "We won't know until we try. But a large part of its success lies with you." Get the parents to realize that their implementation can be a large factor in achieving success. Only after the barometer is implemented consistently over a period of time can its success or failure be truly judged. If it proves not to work despite the parents' and clinician's best efforts, different or additional techniques should be attempted.

Question 4: My child is noncompliant at school. Can this work at school?

Children who are noncompliant in home settings often also have problems with compliance at school. The implementation of the noncompliance barometer in the school requires teacher cooperation. If this can be obtained, it is possible to use the technique in school settings. However, particularly in large classes, the teacher may not be able or unwilling to conduct an individual plan that requires additional effort. Chapter 6 addresses school-related problems, including noncompliance issues.

☐ **Summary**

The non-compliance barometer is a useful technique for helping parents to obtain greater levels of compliance from their children. It establishes an acceptable behavioral standard over a designated period and imposes a fine for acts of noncompliance. If the child stays at or above the standard on the noncompliance barometer, he or she earns a designated reinforcer. Parents implement this technique within a general parental compliance repertoire package. The behavioral standard is altered when success is reliably achieved until a desirable level of compliance is attained. If parents desire, acts of compliance can be the focus of the treatment by using a compliance barometer. A standard acceptable level of compliance behavior is set, which, when achieved, produces a designated reinforcer for the child.

Parent Solutions for School-Related Problems: The Daily Report Card

The following may sound familiar:

> Mrs. F., this is Principal S. at your son's school. Johnny had some trouble this morning. He has refused to do his work in math, and his teacher has had to remove him from the class multiple times. On the last occasion, he became upset and used verbal profanity toward his teacher. She became scared and called my office. He is now in my office, and I am requesting that you come and pick him up. We cannot tolerate such behavior at this school, and I hope that you will straighten this out.

Some parents seek professional help because their child is presenting difficulties such as these in school. Maybe the child has never been sent home or suspended, but the parents keep getting reports and notes from the teacher about unacceptable behavior. These reports may be coming as frequently two to four times a week. The teacher may have questioned the parent's as to what they are going to do about this problem. The school may even be considering placement outside the regular class to "better suit" the child's needs.

These issues are all too common in many families. Clinicians come into frequent contact with families experiencing such problems. In these types

---

Table 1. Factors indicative of need for home-based program

---

1. Has the child been sent home for a behavioral incident? If yes, how many times? Describe the incidents that resulted in suspension or expulsion.
2. Is the child's behavior a source of concern to the teacher? Has such behavior been brought up as a concern during parent-teacher conferences? (Clinicians may need to arrange to speak with the teacher about such concerns if parents consent to disclosure of information.)
3. Has the teacher requested that the parents consult a physician on the possible appropriateness of medications designed to manage child behavior? (This should be a warning sign that all is not well in the classroom.)
4. Have the parents been asked to consent to assessment to determine the child's eligibility for special education services, required in some degree by the problem behaviors demonstrated in the regular classroom?
5. Do the parents feel they need some way to impress their child with the importance of good behavior at school? Have other attempts by the parents to promote good behavior been ineffective? Has counseling been rendered and been found not to result in behavior change at school?

---

of cases, they should consider developing a behavioral plan that provides accountability for the child's school behavior through home-based reinforcement as an adjunct to direct service or individual child therapy.

To determine whether there are issues and concerns with child behaviors at school, the parents should answer the questions in Table 1.

Although there are no hard and fast rules for determining whether a systematic behavioral plan is indicated based on the parent's answers to these interview questions, they can provide a quick picture of the extent of problem behaviors at school. In evaluating the seriousness of a child's school behavior, the professional should lean toward making a decision in favor of implementing a plan if there is a suggestion of problems. For example, the parental interview may create the impression that school personnel are not greatly distressed at the child's behavior currently. The parents may report that their child occasionally is sent to the principal's office. Neither the parents nor the school personnel might see an immediate need for systematic intervention, possibly believing that the child will grow out of it or is just in a phase of adjustment to school life. Situations and conditions change, however. Just because the child's inappropriate behaviors are being tolerated by his second grade teacher does not mean that tolerance will be the case in the coming third, fourth, and fifth grades with new teachers. Using effective child management strategies as a preventive approach is the best course of action parents can take. It is best not to wait to intervene until the child's fifth grade teacher is recommending he be exiled to the planet Jupiter!

A related issue concerns teachers who tolerate inappropriate behaviors. Some parents heap heavy praise on the tolerant teacher for looking past their child's problem behaviors. These teachers, however, are not doing parents or child any favors. "Doing right" would translate into taking such problems seriously enough to develop a systematic behavior plan to effectively reduce the level of problem behavior. Passing that child, with behavior problems intact, to next year's teacher does a service for no one involved (and vested) in the child's future. In the long term, the problem behavior (if left unchanged) will catch up with the child. In hindsight, many parents of older children having continued difficulty with school realize the fallacy of tolerating inattentive or disruptive class behavior when the child was younger. Effective solutions, not merely tolerance or acceptance of misbehavior, are needed for long-term resolution. Teachers who want to be effective agents of behavioral change, not tolerant people who want to pass these problems on to someone else, should be commended.

☐ Parent Questions About School-Related Behavior Problems

Parents may have a number of questions about school-related problems. Some of these possible questions and issues are presented here.

Question 1: My child's teacher phones me frequently about her behavior. What can I do if I'm not in the classroom?

In some cases, once an attempt to modify child behaviors at school becomes unsuccessful, school personnel resort to phone calls home. These teachers and principals think that having the parent aware of the problem behavior at school will result in problem resolution. The underlying assumption on their part is that parents are capable of doing something at home that will ameliorate or eliminate the problem behavior at school. This is usually a poor assumption. Some parents know how to deal with problems at school by setting up home-delivered consequences. With these parents, the "call home" strategy works. In *many, many* other cases, however, parents do not know what to do and may even be seeking professional help for their child's school and home problems. Asking these parents to come up with an effective solution is akin to asking a computer-illiterate person to provide a solution for a programmer who is having difficulty using a particular software program.

Most children can learn to behave more appropriately at school if there is a reinforcement plan that systematically rewards desired appropriate behavior. If the teacher has indicated an unwillingness to monitor appropriate behavior frequently and to dispense reinforcers when they occur, the parents may need to rely on dispensing reinforcers at home. Using home-based consequences for behavior that occurs at school can allow parents to help influence their child's behavior there. To do this, parents need the cooperation of the teacher to track and record one or several simple behaviors a few times each day. The parent should be cautioned not to make enemies with the school (if such has not already happened) to increase the likelihood of teacher cooperation in this venture.

Question 2: I already restrict my child when he brings home bad report cards. Isn't that enough?

Restriction of privileges is a technique many parents rely on in an attempt to exert control over their child's behavior in school. For example, Isaac brings home two C's, three D's, and one F on his report card, and his mother tells him no TV until the next report card. Restricting privileges is often used for report cards only, which can be too long-term a consequence to effect desired behavior change in the child. The following hypothetical scenario illustrates how this discipline technique breaks down:

> Sarah's mother explodes on seeing her daughter's report card, "Sarah, failing every subject but PE, is not acceptable in my book! You're grounded for the rest of the year. That will teach you to take school more seriously." However, Sarah goes to a basketball game two weeks later because her mother felt like she needed a break.

The restriction in this scenario occurs when Sarah brings home bad report card grades. The restriction consequence was designated to be in effect for the rest of the year. If this were carried out, what incentive would Sarah have to perform in school the next day, next week, or subsequent months, since she is already restricted? None! With this strategy, it is no wonder that bad grades are brought home in following semesters, and the parents feel like nothing will work.

The clinician must point out to parents that access to privileges should be made contingent on more short-term behavior, that is, behavior during a single day or week. In this manner, privileges can be provided on a more frequent basis for good behavior. Conversely, loss of privileges results when unacceptable behavior occurs on a given day, and that loss should be effected as soon as possible. Waiting until the report card is brought home is too late. The parents must make the distinction between their prior use of restriction of privileges (contingent on bad grades) and the clinician's proposal about a home-based reinforcement program.

Question 3: I'm tired of the teacher saying I need to be more strict at home. Am I the source of my child's problems at school?

It is unfortunate that some often teachers, principals, and other school staff blame problem behaviors in school on parental discipline policies or the lack thereof. This is not to say that parental discipline policies could not be strengthened in some cases to increase appropriate behaviors and compliance in the home. In many cases, however, the child's undesirable behavior at school could undergo change if stronger *reinforcement* consequences were brought to bear by the teacher for school behavior. In too many cases, the lack of systematic behavioral plans for child classroom behavior is the primary or secondary culprit.

The best way to deal with this question probably is to indicate that it is in no one's interest to blame either party for the problem. Rather, the focus should be on identifying a strategy that can work to solve the problem to everyone's benefit. The parents and teacher should be told that blame and excuses did not result in the desirable outcome up to this point and that it is time to put blame aside and work together to bring the problem behavior under control. With the cooperation of both, the plan being suggested might help.

Question 4: Can my child be having problems because she is "slow"*?

We always assume that when a child misbehaves it is the result of his or her lack of motivation to either behave appropriately or do the work: "Johnny doesn't read because he's lazy." "Phillip gets out of his seat because he's incorrigible." Many people, dismiss the possibility that a child's inappropriate behaviors may be the side effect or result of inadequate skills (i.e., incompetence) in the academic materials. If one considers that the child's inability to perform competently on the academic materials may be a powerful factor, examining the curriculum demands,

---

*The word *slow* is used by many parents because of its preference to other terms, such as *mentally retarded*. I intend no personal attribution in the use of this term toward children with learning difficulties.

which may be too great for the child, or the instructional procedures, which may be ineffective, becomes a relevant strategy.

Clinicians may want to gather information on the child's competence with the academic materials in the class. The parents can bring in work samples or the child can do some homework in the clinician's presence. If the child is having difficulty performing daily classwork, the problem behaviors may be the result of skill deficits in academic capability. Skill deficits must be addressed for any behavior change project to be successful in the long term. The manner in which deficits should be addressed is with more effective instructional material and teaching methods. If this is the case, the parents may need to seek help in obtaining effective instructional procedures for their child (if such is not in the clinician's repertoire).

Question 5: Will my child grow out of this stage?

With young children, parents are often told that the child's inappropriate behavior may just be reflective of the stage of development and that the problem behavior will disappear with age. This is the "wait and see" approach: "Johnny's just 3 years old, he's in the terrible 3's. Don't worry, he'll grow out of it!"

What are the implications of this analysis? The logic of this approach suggests that once Johnny turns 4 years old, the source of concern will disappear. This is doubtful. "Wait and see" might be an appealing approach because it does not take a lot of effort or expertise on anyone's part.

In most cases, children do not automatically demonstrate improved behavior just because they grow older. What seems to happen is that as the child ages; parents and teachers implement discipline strategies that effect change in undesirable behaviors. A tantrum by a 3-year-old preschool child may result in his getting a cookie in the grocery store; therefore, tantrums become more prevalent when the child wants something. But by the age of 7, tantrums no longer have the desired result so they become less frequent.

But what if the consequences for tantrums are not altered as the child gets older? What if a 7-year-old throws loud and intense tantrums? Should the parents wait a year or two to see if the behavior changes on its own?

A better question might be, Why take the risk of waiting?" Implementing an effective program only serves to add insurance to the possibility of succeeding anyway. Identifying potential and current problems early in life and solving them can certainly lead to less heartache and headache as the child gets older. If they could comprehend the consequences of their behavior at an early age, most children would choose not to behave inappropriately in classrooms or to complete only minimal amounts of work. The problem is that most children (and sometimes parents and teachers) do not take into account the long-term consequences of such behaviors. Implementing a systematic program to reduce school misbehavior early in life is likely to have superior benefits to the "wait and see" strategy.

☐ Brief Description

The daily report card provides a means for parents to reward appropriate school behavior each day. It provides yes/no information on selected appropriate or inappropriate behaviors. If the child had a good schoolday (the criteria for which would be designated earlier) as verified by the daily report card, parents provide the child with previously agreed-on extra privileges later that day. If the child did not have a good day, those extra privileges are withheld.

☐ Empirical Basis for the Daily Report Card

Children were experiencing behavior problems at school long before the present generation. Parents or grandparents often relate how problem behaviors were dealt with in the "good old days." As the story goes, teachers used to walk softly and carry a big stick, ruler, or whatever else was handy. The junior high school I attended in Florida used paddling as a discipline technique in the mid 1960s, and this is still a method used in schools in some states. However, discipline tactics have largely changed over the years. When some schools discarded the more seemingly punitive approaches, *effective* alternatives to take their place were lacking. As teachers began to lose control of behavior in their classes, they would often turn to parents and say, "What are you going to do about your child?"

The need for a technique that allows parents to effectively monitor the school behavior of their child was brought to the attention of researchers in the Bureau of Child Research and Department of Human Development at University of Kansas (Bailey, Wolf, & Phillips, 1970). They wanted to design a system that would be feasible for the teacher to use to monitor the child's behavior in the classroom. The parent, in turn, would use this

Table 2.   Sample daily report card

1. Studied whole period?	Yes	No
2. Obeyed class rules?	Yes	No

information to determine whether the child should get special privileges. They tested their system on five children who lived in a group home called Achievement Place. These children were reported to be difficult for teachers to control. For example, one boy had been sent to the principal's office for disrupting class so often during the previous school year that he was suspended twice and held back a grade level as a result. Another child assaulted not only other students but the teacher as well (this was in the late 1960's; this scenario could describe many adolescents in to-day's schools).

The researchers designed a child management system they termed ''home-based reinforcement'' and implemented it during the summer school class that the five boys were taking. The daily report card system focused on reducing the boys' current high levels of rule violations and increasing the low rate of class study behavior. Everyday, each child brought a report card to school. At the end of the day, the teacher filled out each boy's card by merely answering *yes* or *no* to each of the two questions shown in Table 2.

If the child brought home a daily report card from the teacher that had *yes* marked to both questions, he had access to three significant privileges that afternoon or evening. However, if he had a *no* marked to either question, he lost access to those privileges for that day. This system of tracking each child's behavior was easy to deploy. The teacher merely had to take time at the end of the day to circle the appropriate response for each question and then give it back to the student in a sealed envelope.

The system certainly sounds doable, but did it work? Fortunately, the researchers found that it had a marked improvement on each child's classroom behavior. When the daily report card system was implemented, levels of study behavior occurred increased while rates of rule violations decreased for each child. The daily report card system was tested with other students, and similar positive results on student performance and behavior were obtained.

☐ **Components of the Daily Report Card Program**

There are six components to the daily report card program:

1. Gaining cooperation of parent and teacher

2. Identification of specific school problem behaviors that will be targeted
3. Determination of how such behavior will be tracked by teacher
4. Collection of baseline data on problem behavior.
5. Identification of the acceptable behavioral standard for earning home privileges
6. Implementation of the system

Component 1: Gaining Cooperation of Parents and Teacher

Obviously, the first step is to determine whether the parents and teacher are committed to working on a plan that would involve some effort on both their parts. One hopes that both are agreeable to the basic premise of the plan. At this stage, the clinician can meet with the parties individually (if parents give consent for a meeting with school personnel). The clinician outlines the basic components of the system but indicates that he or she cannot provide specifics until more information is collected. Possible privileges to be earned or lost by the child on a daily or weekly basis could also be discussed. In meeting with the teacher, the clinician explains how the daily report card system works and attempts to establish a mutually agreed-on preliminary system to track the problem behaviors of concern.

Component 2: Identification of Targeted Problem Behavior

Once parent and teacher cooperation is obtained, the next step is to identify the targeted school problem behaviors. A child may exhibit numerous bad behaviors in the classroom. In most cases, the clinician jointly decides with the parents and teacher which behaviors will be targeted for the system. Examples of possible problem behaviors to be tracked are rule violations, disruptive behavior, profanity, and unauthorized chatting.

In some cases, the clinician and parents may want to track *appropriate* behaviors, with an obvious interest in having them occur more often. Appropriate school behaviors that could be considered for tracking include completion of classwork, attending to teacher-presented instructions, compliance with requests, and completion of homework.

The hypothetical example of Johnny, an 8-year-old boy in third grade, and his parents illustrates how to collectively determine the target behaviors to be tracked.

After the clinician has met with the teachers and the parents separately and has become familiar with the presenting child behavior

---

Table 3. Target behaviors

Student Name: Johnny F.   Date: 1/15

Problem behaviors to be tracked:
1. Refusal to engage in assigned work—any occurrence of verbal or physical refusing to engage in reading or writing tasks
2. Profanity toward teacher—any occurrence of profane words directed toward the teacher, usually in response to a teacher's command or instruction

Appropriate behaviors to be tracked
    None

Signatures:

Teacher	Mrs. V.
Principal	Mrs. L.
Parent	Mrs. F.
Parent	Mr. F.
Clinician	Dr. R.

---

problem, the clinician, parents, teacher, and school principal meet at Johnny's school. At this meeting, various problem behaviors are advanced: (1) refusal to do work, (2) use of profanity, (3) inattention to teacher-presented instructions, and (4) lack of cooperative play during recess. After much discussion and input from all persons present, the clinician proposes that only two of the most critical school problems be initially targeted—refusal (either verbal or physical) to engage in assigned work and profanity toward teacher. While inattention to teacher instructions and poor cooperative play skills are problems, the clinician convinced everyone that initially targeting too many problems might be too demanding for any intervention to produce success.

With slight reluctance, school personnel and the parents agree with the clinician on the selection of these two targeted behaviors. It takes a lot of convincing on the clinician's part to sell the proposed plan to the school personnel and the parents, who believe that an intervention worthy of implementation is one that makes all problems disappear tomorrow (or the next day at the latest). To allay the parents' and teacher's skepticism, the clinician indicates that a separate behavior management program would be written for other problem behaviors soon. Table 3 presents a form that documents the agreed-on target behaviors for Johnny. A similar table can be constructed for general use.

Table 4.   Example of a daily report card

===

Tracking exact Frequency: Physical Education Class

Date: 3/13
Child: Ron R.

Target behavior:
Aggression (or attempts) against other children during PE
Instruction for recording: Each time an instance of aggression occurs, circle the next number.

Frequency

①	②	3	4	5	6

Component 3: Identification of How the Targeted Behaviors Will Be Tracked

Once the targeted behaviors have been identified and agreed on, how they will be tracked is of utmost importance. There are many methods for tracking child behaviors, but only three methods are reasonable for school personnel and situations: (1) exact frequency counts, (2) occurrence/nonoccurrence of behavior, and (3) estimated frequency of occurrence.

Exact Frequency Count

In some cases, if the behavior is fairly infrequent, the teacher may be able to track its exact occurrence by counting its frequency across the schoolday. For example, aggressive behavior, although a serious behavior problem, does not usually occur with great frequency. If a child is aggressive only one or two times a day, and the occurrence of an aggressive act is fairly obvious, the teacher may be able to track the exact frequency of its occurrence. The data sheet in Table 4 illustrates a daily report card that uses the exact frequency method of tracking a targeted school problem behavior involving aggression toward other students during physical education class.

The child's aggression is being tracked for a specific time period (PE). Because aggression (or attempts) is apparent to anyone observing the child, the PE teacher has agreed to this system of tracking aggression by recording actual occurrences. All he does is circle the next number at

Table 5.   Tracking three behaviors

Time Period	Not Engaged in Reading a Book		Unauthorized Blurting Out		Out of Seat	
9:00–9:15	O	(NO)	O	(NO)	(O)	NO
9:15–9:30	O	(NO)	(O)	NO	O	(NO)
9:30–9:45	O	(NO)	O	(NO)	O	(NO)
9:45–10:00	(O)	NO	(O)	NO	O	(NO)
10:00–10:15	(O)	NO	(O)	NO	(O)	NO
10:15–10:30	(O)	NO	(O)	NO	O	(NO)

O, occurrence; NO, nonoccurrence.

each occurrence (maximum six episodes in one period). The teacher uses a new daily report card sheet each day. On this particular day, Ron F was aggressive twice during the PE period.

Occurrence/Nonoccurrence of Behavior

The more behaviors one wishes to track, the less probable it is that the teacher will be able to record the exact frequency of each behavior. A less time-consuming tracking system is needed (and appreciated). A system that determines the occurrence or nonoccurrence of a behavior makes better sense when tracking multiple behaviors. The teacher is merely required to record whether the targeted behaviors occurred (either once or multiple times) or did not occur at all.

For example, an occurrence/nonoccurrence tracking system might break up the schoolday into time periods. This could be half days, 2-hour blocks, 1-hour blocks, or even half-hour blocks. Of course, the shorter the time periods are, the more labor-intensive this tracking system is for the teacher, since he or she must record behavior on the data sheet after each time period.

An example of tracking three behaviors (not reading a book, unauthorized blurting out, and being out of seat) in terms of their occurrence or nonoccurrence every 15 minutes in a morning reading period of about 90 minutes is given in Table 5. This data sheet requires the teacher to determine whether each of the three behaviors occurred (one or more times) or did not occur in each 15-minute period. The data indicate that the child had at least one occurrence of not being engaged in reading a book in three of six 15-minute intervals, of unauthorized blurting out in two of six intervals, and of being out of his seat in four of six intervals.

Table 6.   Elizabeth's estimated daily report card: Daydreaming behavior

Date: 3/23

Frequency Estimate
Category 1—estimated occurrence of 1–4 times
Category 2—estimated occurrence of 5–10 times
Category 3—estimated occurrence of more than 10 times

Class Period	Category 1	Category 2	Category 3
Period 1	(1–4)	5–10	Over 10
Period 2	1–4	(5–10)	Over 10
Period 3	1–4	(5–10)	Over 10
Period 4	1–4	5–10	(Over 10)
Period 5	1–4	5–10	(Over 10)

Estimated Frequency of Behavior

As discussed earlier, if the behavior occurs fairly frequently, the teacher may not have time to count every occurrence of the behavior. Further, the previous method of scoring the behavior as occurring (or not) in an interval can be imprecise. In these cases, a system that involves estimated frequency of behavior can be useful as the method of tracking the behavior.

The teacher estimates the rate of occurrence of the targeted behavior at the end of each designated interval by circling the category that he or she thinks best describes the level of behavior. For example, one can estimate the frequency of the behavior across an entire day according to three categories—zero to two occurrences, three to seven occurrences, or eight or more occurrences. The teacher would merely identify at the end of the day which category is most representative of the estimated rate for that day. Or, a frequency estimate can be made across a number of 2-hour blocks. Within each 2-hour block, the teacher estimates the frequency of occurrence.

The example in Table 6 illustrates how Elizabeth's daydreaming (high-frequency behavior) is tracked using an estimate of its frequency across the five 1-hour periods of the schoolday. Elizabeth's teacher circled one of the above three categories (i.e., 1 to 4, 5 to 10, over 10) for each period (time would be designated), based on her estimate of the frequency of the behavior during each period. As an illustrative example, on 3/23, the teacher estimated that Elizabeth daydreamed somewhere between 1 and 4 times during period 1 and between 5 and 10 times during period 2.

She circles the appropriate column as soon as the period is over. The teacher estimates the frequency of daydreaming after each period on the basis of her observation. Although this method is not as precise as an actual frequency count, it can be helpful (and certainly more feasible for teachers to use) for tracking behaviors that are fairly frequent.

In summary, one of the three tracking systems is selected and forms the basis of the daily report card that goes home to the parents. The data contained on the daily report card are used by the parent to determine whether privileges are earned or lost that night. Several precautions should be taken to ensure the information on the daily report card always gets home. First, the teacher should keep a copy of the daily report card in case it "gets lost" before the parents have a chance to examine the data. Second, sealing it in an envelope reduces the likelihood that data will be altered by the child before been seen by the parents. Finally, the teacher may periodically communicate the results on the daily report card to the parents over the phone.

Component 4: Collection of Baseline Data on Problem Behavior

Before implementing the system, the clinician needs to ensure that enough information is available on the problem behavior being targeted. This requires that the tracking system be used without reinforcement for a time. Collecting 1 to 2 weeks of baseline data in the classroom typically allows the clinician to determine the initial acceptable standard for reinforcement. The clinician can then select standard that is likely to produce success in the early phase of the plan.

An example of such baseline data is presented in Table 7. These present the estimated frequency of Elizabeth's daydreaming according to category (i.e., frequency estimates of 1 to 4 were category 1, estimates of 5 to 10 were category 2, and estimates of more than 10 were category 3). In this manner, one can add the categories across the five periods of the day to obtain a summed score. According to Table 7, on 3/21, Elizabeth's summed score was 10, whereas on 3/26 it was 9. The range of the summed scores across 5 days was 8 (low) to 11 (high). These baseline data can then be used to plan the intervention.

In some cases, the parents or the teacher may object to the initial collection of baseline information. Their reason for not wanting to collect such information is that the behavior problem is of such severe nature that the plan must begin immediately. In most circumstances, this is not the case, and the clinician can educate parents and teachers about the necessity for baseline data collection and its function in the design of the

Table 7.   Elizabeth's daily report card: Weekly results of daydreaming frequency estimate

Category	Estimated Frequency of Daydreaming
1	Between 1 and 4
2	Between 5 and 10
3	More than 10

Period	3/21	3/22	3/23	3/26	3/27
1	1	1	1	1	2
2	2	1	2	1	1
3	1	1	2	2	1
4	3	3	3	2	2
5	3	3	3	3	2
Sum	10	9	11	9	8

behavioral plan. He or she can also point out that 1 or 2 more weeks of the problem behavior occurring is certainly minor in comparison with the weeks, months, or sometimes years that the problem behavior has been occurring until this point. Nevertheless, in some circumstances, the clinician should be sensitive to the fact that some referred problem behaviors are of such a severe nature as to warrant immediate intervention. If the child is assaulting teachers or students, immediate intervention is appropriate. In most other cases, however, collecting baseline data is instrumental to the next component and should be collected.

Component 5: Identification of Acceptable Behavioral Standard for Earning Home Privileges

With the baseline information, the clinician can begin to determine the initial acceptable behavioral standard for earning home privileges. To do this, the baseline data are examined and a standard computed that will allow the child to gain privileges 50% to 70% of the time on the basis of the baseline data alone.

Table 8 is hypothetical daily report card illustrating how the initial acceptable behavioral standard is identified from baseline data. The data are from the five periods in the schoolday. The teacher circled an occurrence each period in which Phil used profanity toward her. In examining

Table 8.   Phil's profanity toward teacher: Occurrence/nonoccurrence method

	Day of Week				
Period/Day	M	T	W	Th	F
1	◎	◎	◎	◎	O
2	O	O	O	O	O
3	◎	O	O	◎	O
4	O	O	O	◎	O
5	O	O	O	O	O
Total score per day	2	1	1	3	0

these data, the clinician notes that profanity occurred at least once in two periods on Monday, one period on Tuesday, one period on Wednesday, three periods on Thursday, and not at all on Friday. Based on these data if the clinician selects no occurrences of profanity as the standard for reinforcement, only 1 of 5 days would result in privileges. This low access to privileges for Phil may not be strong enough to begin to affect his misbehavior. Realizing this, a wise clinician determines that a successful day is a daily report card of one or less periods in which an occurrence of profanity was recorded. This standard would result in Phil's getting privileges 3 days a week. On days like Monday and Thursday, he would forego privileges at home. It may take some convincing of the parents and teacher that one or fewer periods is a better initial standard than no periods at all, especially with Phil's targeted behavior. The teacher can be told that as the first occurrence of profanity is scored, the child can be warned, providing some consequences for the first occurrence.

The clinician can tell the parents and teacher that once success has been achieved with this initial standard, the standard can be altered to become more stringent. Phil would then have to forego any instance of profanity during the day to earn home privileges. The parents and teachers must keep in mind that there is an overall ultimate goal that the program is heading toward, and changes in the behavioral standard are made as a function of gradual improvement in the child's behavior. An example of the clinician's meeting with the parents and teacher to set the initial behavioral standard follows for Elizabeth, the daydreamer, follows.

Clinician: As I examine this week's data, [Table 9], I see that Elizabeth's summed score across all five periods ranges from 8 to 11 across the 5

Table 9.   Baseline data for Elizabeth's daydreaming

Summed Score Across Five Periods

Date	
3/21	10
3/33	9
3/23	11
3/24	9
3/25	8
	Average X = 9.4

days that you collected these baseline data. Thank you once again, Ms. Ramirez, for your efforts. Now it's time to make those efforts pay off.

Teacher: Thank you. Anything to help Elizabeth. She's such a darling child, and very bright. If she can daydream less, her work should improve dramatically. I'm so hopeful.

Clinician: There are two things we need to establish today. First is the designation of the initial standard for a successful day of "less day-dreaming." In other words, at what score will we consider Elizabeth to have had a bad or good day, as far as daydreaming less in class? The second area we need to discuss is the privileges she will earn when she has a successful day and, consequently, the loss of such privileges for an unsuccessful day.

Parent: Okay, let's do this. I want to thank you, Ms. Ramirez, for all you've done. Really. *[Clinician may need to prompt parent a priori to provide praise for teachers' efforts during meeting.]*

Clinician: I'd like to suggest that we start with a summed score of 9 or lower as the standard for a successful day. Based on the baseline data, Elizabeth should be able to achieve this daily goal readily. Ms. Ramirez will continue sending home the daily report card, filled out at the bottom with the sum of the categories for that day. If the sum is 9 or below, Ms. Ramirez will place a star on the card for that day, which means Elizabeth earned privileges. If the sum is 10 or higher, Elizabeth will not earn privileges that night. After each period, Ms. Ramirez will estimate the frequency of daydreaming and record the category (1, 2, or 3) on a separate card. Elizabeth will be allowed to see that card so that she can keep track of how well she's doing. Does that sound doable?

Teacher: Yes, it can certainly fit into my schedule.

Parent: What should I do when the card comes home?

Table 10.   Three weeks of summed scores

Week 1   Range of summed scores   6–10 (lost out 1 day)
Week 2—Range of summed scores—6–9 (did not lose a day)
Week 3—Range of summed scores—7–9 (did not lose a day)

Clinician: Good follow-up question! If Elizabeth has a star, give her praise as access to the privileges we talked about earlier. She would earn the right to go to bed at 9:00 p.m., rather than her normal 8:30 p.m. bedtime. But, no star—bed at 8:30. We will evaluate this program in 3 weeks. If we do not get a change in daydreaming from the baseline, we'll look to see whether the privileges can be changed or made more powerful.

Three weeks pass, and Elizabeth's mother brings in the data shown in Table 10.

Clinician: Wow. This looks great! What's your impression, Ms. Ramirez?

Teacher: I'm really happy with Elizabeth's effort. She's missed getting a star only 1 day during the past 3 weeks. She's been super!

Parent: Yes, I'm really pleased with her as well.

Clinician: Do you both feel like we should set a more stringent standard? Is her daydreaming still getting in the way of her work?

Teacher: Yes, in some periods, I would say so. When she gets a 1 category, that's a good period for her. But every once in awhile she gets a 3, and then there's been too much daydreaming for that period. If she could stay between categories 1 and 2, that would be great!

Clinician: Okay, that's good information. It looks like she can reliably hit a 6 or 7 summed score. Let's make the new standard 7 or less. She earns a star (and subsequent privileges) with a daily score of 7 or less. After 3 weeks, we can come together again and see if we need any changes to this new standard. How does that sound?

Parent: Great, I'm excited. I have so many hopes for her now. Thank you, Ms. Ramirez, for everything.

Teacher: This has been great. I wish we could do this for some other children in my class, who really need something like this.

☐ Questions About Implementing the Daily Report Card

Question 1: What are some examples of rewards, incentives, or privileges that parents can use in the home?

On learning that a reinforcement plan is being considered, parents often jump to the conclusion that additional rewards or privileges are involved. Eight of 10 times, the privileges or rewards to be used are already being given or provided to the child but are *not contingent on the child's behavior*. The clinician, through parental interview, identifies possible privileges and incentives that could be used in the system (that are currently given noncontingently). For example, many kids play Nintendo each day without having to earn such a privilege. The clinician might point out to the parent that playing Nintendo can be a privilege available to the child as a function of the daily report card.

The following illustration provides an example of such a contingency for Nintendo time: "If you have no more than one period (out of six periods) with a misbehavior marked (being out of seat, rule violations) during the day, you earn 45 minutes of Nintendo time after homework is completed that evening."

This use of Nintendo as the earned privilege means that the child cannot play Nintendo on days when the criterion is exceeded. Convince the parent of the need to remove Nintendo privileges on that day. This is not to say that all activities and privileges need to be made a part of the daily report card system. But those that are selected should have a powerful impact on the child's behavior. Table 11 presents a number of privileges the clinician and the parent might use as the reward for a successful day (or week).

Question 2: What happens if the child has an unacceptable day? Should we be allowed to remove additional privileges?

The daily report card indicates whether the home privileges are accessed or lost on a given day. Some parents may be tempted to remove a number of additional privileges not agreed on as a function of an unacceptable day. In the earlier example, Nintendo is lost if the criterion is exceeded. It did not say that the child would go to bed 3 hours early and lose dinner. In some cases, parents "creatively add on" to that which was originally discussed. They should be reminded that they need to stick with the agreed-on privileges and not invent additional ones on the spur of the moment. If possible, the parent should agree not to alter the system unless the clinician has been consulted first. If the data suggest that additional

---

Table 11.   Possible privileges to be used in daily report card system

---

Possible privileges to earn (daily)
   Extra TV, videos, Nintendo
   Special breakfast of child's choice (e.g., pancakes instead of just cereal)
   Later bedtime
   Less homework (if teacher agrees)
   Getting out of one or more chores
   Money (almost always assured to be a powerful motivator)

Possible privileges to earn (weekly)
   Trip to mall
   Trip to swimming pool
   No Saturday afternoon chores
   Video rental of choice on Friday or Saturday night
   Special outing
   Money

---

privileges should be added or removed to effect the desired change in behavior, that needs to be a joint decision made by the clinician and the parents.

Question 3: What if this system doesn't work?

The clinician must indicate to the parent that the system may not work in some cases for a number of possible reasons. First, the privileges identified may not be powerful enough. If this is the case, simply identifying alternative incentives and privileges and using them on the system could be the solution.

A second possible factor is that the behavioral standard for earning privileges may be set too high. If this is the case, as demonstrated by weeks of failure to achieve the standard, the solution is merely to lower the standard for a time until the child is successful and then to gradually raise the standard later.

Question 4: Will this help the child's grades?

If low grades or poor performance are due to the child's lack of motivation to behave appropriately in school and to attend to instruction, a daily report card system may help his or her grades. If the low grades are due to academic skill deficits, however, this system probably will not effect a change in the child's grades, and a further examination of the child's skill and instructional presentation needs to occur.

Question 5: What should the parents do if the material covered in class is too difficult for the child?

If the low performance seems to be due to skill deficits, it is strongly recommended that the parents meet with the teacher and administrator to identify these areas of concern and to determine what *instructional* solutions can be implemented. The class may be above the child's abilities. So an analysis of the child's strengths and weaknesses in the curriculum may be warranted. If instructional methods and curriculum are not part of the clinician's repertoire, the child should be referred to someone who is skilled in these areas. The parents might also consider additional tutoring or home instruction to improve such skills.

☐ Summary

This chapter has dealt with an area of concern for many parents—school-related child problem behaviors. Parents do not have to feel helpless in attempting to deal with problem behaviors that occur at school. Rather, with the cooperation of the teacher and the use of the daily report card system, school problems can be tackled. With parents and teachers working cooperatively, an untenable situation can often be changed, and many of these children can profit more from attending school.

The Effective Use of Time-Out for Disruptive Behavior

What's been said about time-out?

Parent 1: I've used time-out, but it doesn't work. My child thinks it's funny. He doesn't take me seriously!

Parent 2: My child won't stay in time-out. She keeps getting up.

Parent 3: My child likes time-out. It doesn't work for me. I've tried it off and on, and it just doesn't work. I need something else.

Therapist 1: Time-out does not work in some cases. When parents use time-out, they violate a bond between parent and child, and the mistrust the child develops as a result has far-reaching implications.

Therapist 2: Time-out is based on a stick-and-carrot approach. Children are not rabbits. They need a parent who provides positive discipline.

Time-out has received a lot of bad press. Although it is a frequently used strategy to deal with a wide variety of child problems, it has often been misused and abused. Nevertheless, it is one of the most often studied, empirically validated, effective techniques in the research literature. In fact, time-out was one of the techniques to receive early empirical support in behavior therapy.

Time-out has been demonstrated to be highly effective with a variety of children, for a variety of problem behaviors, and in a variety of settings. The presentation of time-out in this chapter is geared toward disruptive

Table 1.   Screening questions for child behavior during playtime

_____	Does the child engage in disruptive behavior during unstructured or play periods? If so, what specific behaviors?
_____	Tantrums
_____	Throws toys
_____	Aggressive against other children
_____	Does not take turns
_____	Runs in inappropriate areas in the house
_____	Other
_____	Do you find yourself frequently intervening during the child's play to stop his or her disruptive behavior?
_____	Do you feel ineffective in supervising your child's play?
_____	Is your child's disruptive behavior more frequent or severe than other children's behaviors?

behavior in situations in which compliance with parental requests or commands is not an issue (see Chapters 5 and 6). If done right, time-out can be an extremely powerful tool. Hence, its inclusion here. Time-out can be applied in home and community settings when young children are engaged in desirable activities, such as television, games, or other unstructured times.

To determine whether a time-out intervention is needed for a problem area, the questions in Table 1 can be of use.

There are no hard and fast rules for determining whether the family is in need of help in this area. However, the clinician may need to determine whether the child's behavior is in need of change or whether the parent unrealistic in his or her expectation for good behavior during unstructured times. The following three factors need to be considered in making this decision: the age of the child, the presence or absence of reasonable rules, and the type of problem behavior.

Obviously, the younger the child, the greater the type and number of misbehaviors. Developmental issues need to be taken into account when considering the need for intervention. A related factor is the rules established by the parents for unstructured or play periods. Are the rules reasonable for the age of the child and the setting? Do the rules set the child up for failure?

The type of problem behaviors exhibited also affect the decision to intervene. For example, if the child is hitting other children, this disruptive behavior usually constitutes a problem. However, if the 4-year-old child occasionally runs in the house, provided the running is not producing another more dangerous or disruptive condition (e.g., runs into the hot stove), it may not signify the need for systematic intervention. In consultation with parents, the clinician can consider these factors when contemplating the possibility of intervention.

Time-out can be an effective technique for a variety of disruptive behaviors. A study using time-out effectively with a number of young children is presented later.

☐ Brief Description

Time-out is a technique that removes the child from a reinforcing and preferable activity as a consequence for a specific disruptive behavior in the home. It is used by the parent each time the target misbehavior occurs. The child is placed in an area that is void of toys or materials and is required to sit (or stay) for some period of time. He or she is released from time-out when the release criteria have been met. The parent praises the child for engaging in appropriate behavior when he or she rejoins the activity or group.

☐ Empirical Basis for Time-Out

Day care centers are a setting in which disruptive behavior needs to be handled. Researchers at the University of Kansas tested the efficacy of a time-out procedure on children attending the Toddlers Center in Lawrence, Kansas (Porterfield, Herbert-Jackson, & Risley, 1976). The children ranged in age from 12 to 36 months. Except for 2 children who had physical handicaps, the 26 preschool children had no special problems.

Initially, the researchers requested that the caregivers use redirection when a child was being disruptive to determine whether it worked. Redirection is an often-used technique to handle disruptive behavior, but its effectiveness is rarely studied (or questioned for that matter). The caregivers would respond to each disruption by describing the inappropriateness of the behavior to the child and then redirecting him or her to an alternate toy. For example, if one child hit another child, the caregiver might say to the offender, "No, Renaldo, you're not supposed to hit other children. Come over here and play with these blocks."

The caregivers were then taught how to use a special form of time-out designed by the researchers called "contingent observation." When the child engaged in a disruptive behavior, the caregiver would follow these five steps:

1. Caregiver described the form of the behavior and its inappropriateness to the child and told him or her what the appropriate behavior would have been in that situation.
2. Caregiver moved the child to the periphery of the activity area, sitting him or her on the floor without materials and asking him or her to observe the appropriate behavior of other children.
3. If the child had been watching for a brief but unspecified amount of time (less than a minute), the caregiver asked the child if he or she was ready to rejoin the activity.
4. If the child indicated yes by nodding his or her head and getting up or verbalizing that he or she was ready to return to the group, the child was allowed to do so. If the child did not respond or responded negatively, the caregiver told him or her to continue sitting and watching until he or she was ready.
5. When the child returned to the group and demonstrated appropriate behavior, the caregiver gave him or her positive attention.

A hypothetical scenario of the application of contingent observation may have looked something like this:

> The caregiver says,
> "Johnny, you do not throw blocks against the wall. You should stack them or build something with them." Caregiver takes Johnny to the periphery of the play area and sits him down. "Johnny, you're to sit here and watch the other children as they play with blocks by building things." After 30 seconds have elapsed and the child has been watching attentively, the caregiver approaches Johnny and says, "Are you ready to return to the group and play appropriately?" Johnny nods his head and says, "Yes." He returns to the group and as soon as he goes to the blocks and plays appropriately with them, the caregiver goes over to him and says, "Nice building, Johnny! *That's* the way to play with blocks."

These steps were used for all behaviors except fussing or crying. Because toddlers may be fussy or may cry for a reason, the caregiver was taught to comfort the child for a brief time and attempt to get him or her interested in an activity. If the child's fussing or crying did not subside within this period, he or she was taken to a beanbag chair placed at the edge of the playroom to sit and rest until he or she felt better. The child could return to the play activity whenever he or she was calm and ready.

If a child was extremely disruptive during the contingent observation procedure and remained so for a few minutes, if the crying or screaming was so loud that it disrupted other children's play, or if the child refused to sit quietly on the periphery, he or she was then taken to the "quiet place." When a caregiver determined that a child should be taken to the quiet place, this was explained to him or her and he or she was told that when ready (by being quiet), he or she could return to the periphery and sit and quietly watch.

In contrast to the redirection technique, contingent observation was extremely effective in reducing both disruption and aggression for each child. For example, hourly disruptive behaviors per child ranged from a little over three to almost eight incidents or disruptions per hour when the caregiver used redirection. During contingent observation, the rate of disruptions per child ranged from one to a maximum of three per hour.

Before the components of time-out are delineated, it is imperative that the conditions under which time-out is clinically indicated, and conditions under which it is not indicated, be presented. Too often, the prescription of time-out for certain problems under certain contexts is incorrect. The following section considers the clinical indicators for using time-out.

☐ When to Use Time-Out

Time-out is used by parents for a variety of behaviors under many different contexts. However, it is not clinically indicated in all circumstances. If used under conditions in which it is not indicated, time-out will reliably fail. Its use has a place in home and community settings if the activity the child is engaged in is pleasurable, preferred, and highly reinforcing to the child (e.g., playtime, video or TV time, eating dessert).

In most cases, children love to play. Therefore, using time-out when the child is engaged in play would provide an effective consequence for misbehavior in that the child would be removed from such an activity.

In contrast, one would not remove a child from an activity that he or she cared little for or actively avoided. For example, in many school classrooms, time-out is used as a consequence for misbehaviors. Does removal of the child for misbehavior from an academic activity (that the child may not be terribly interested in) serve as a powerful consequence for misbehaviors? Doubtful. What is the child losing? The opportunity to do math?

Table 2 lists some circumstances in which time-out should not be used (based on the preference and dislikes of many children).

In the case of a child doing homework, one could see that using time-out for misbehaviors during this activity, as the sole technique, would feed into that bad behavior. The child would be removed from homework (which he or she did not want to do) and would learn to misbehave to get out of homework. So what if the child has to sit for awhile? It beats having to do homework. The use of time-out in the other examples in

---

Table 2.   Circumstances in which time-out should not be used

---

1. The child is to do chores (especially if he or she dislikes the particular chore).
2. The child is supposed to be doing homework.
3. The child is supposed to be getting ready for bed.
4. The child is a picky eater during mealtime.

Table 2 would have a similar effect: the child might misbehave to get out of the undesirable activity.

If the clinician and parents wish to use time-out in a circumstance similar to one of those in Table 2, a tangible reinforcer should be used for appropriate behavior. If the child is provided an incentive for completing the assigned chore or completing homework, being removed from the activity is an effective consequence for disruptive behavior. This example illustrates this.

> Mrs. G. had used time-out when her 6-year-old daughter, Alessandra, threw tantrums when it was time to do Saturday chores. Time-out in this situation simply did not work. Alessandra still has tantrums, and chores are often not completed. Mrs. G. decides to provide a powerful, tangible incentive for completed chores. If Alessandra can finish her three Saturday chores before 10:00 a.m., Mrs. G. will take her to the park to play on the swings or jungle gym that morning. She will still use time-out as a consequence for any tantrum behavior. Many weeks later, Alessandra is completing her chores regularly. Also, if she does have a tantrum during this period, time-out works well. She has rarely had a tantrum since the first 2 weeks. One Saturday, because she was in time-out for a long time, she did not finish her chores. Subsequently, she did not get to go to the park. Since that Saturday, she has not missed going to the park.

In this scenario, when the incentive to complete Saturday chores was made powerful, the child did not want to go to time-out and therefore avoided having a tantrum. This is quite a contrast to her willingness to go to time-out before, when all that resulted was a temporary removal from Saturday chores.

☐ Components and Description of Time-Out

The five components of effective time-out are as follows:

1. Specification of the relationship (i.e., contingency) between occurrence of target child behavior and time-out

2. Specification of a minimum length of the time-out period
3. Specification of the place where child will be removed to
4. Specification of release criteria from time-out
5. Catching the child being good

Component 1: Specifiying the Contingency

One of the major mistakes many parents commit when they use time-out is not to specify a contingency between time-out and a specific behavior. Rather, parents will implement a time-out at some point along the continuum of escalating child behavior. The implementation of time out often looks like this:

> Frieda refuses to put her toy back in the toy box. Her mother says that she is going to be very upset if Frieda does not get cracking and put the toy away. Frieda throws the toy, and it hits the wall. Her mother screams at her, "I said to put the toy in the toy box. That doesn't mean throw it! Are you hard of hearing?" Frieda cries and runs out of play area with another toy, whereupon she dumps it in the garbage can and then laughs. Frieda's mother asks her to pick it up out of the garbage can. Frieda refuses and hits her mom. Her mother then says "That's enough! I've had enough!" and puts Frieda in a chair, saying, "You're in time-out."

In this example, Frieda exhibited multiple instances of disruptive behavior before time-out was put into effect. Time-out was not effected until the last instance of disruptive behavior, which involved hitting.

Why is it incorrect not to pinpoint a specific problem behavior to produce time-outs? If a specific behavior is not targeted for time-out, the child is unsure about what behavior produces time-out. He or she will often engage in an escalation of disruptive behavior, not knowing where the line will be drawn. Additionally, the consistency rule stressed throughout this book is violated when time-out is not designated and used for each occurrence of a specific behavior.

Inconsistent application of time-out often results from varying parental tolerance of disruptive behavior as a function of the time of day and parental mood. The parent may say, "At times, I get so fed up with Johnny, I just put him in the corner. But that doesn't seem to work, because when he comes out 20 minutes later he's back to making me upset again." One can see that the use of time-out in this circumstance is not contingent on or consistent with any specific behavior. Rather, it rests with the parent's tolerance level at a given time.

The clinician's first step is to teach the parents to specify what form of disruptive behavior should result, every time, in time-out. For example,

Table 3.   Behavior and consequences

Behavioral Incident	Consequence
1. Johnny hits sister.	Time-out
2. Johnny hugs mother.	No time-out*
3. Johnny yells for water.	No time-out*
4. Johnny throws ball at brother.	Time-out
5. Johnny kicks brother.	Time-out
6. Johnny cries when brother takes toy away.	No time-out*

*Parent could use some other technique.

the clinician and the parent could identify physical aggression toward siblings as the targeted behavior. They agree that time-out will not be used for other behaviors (for now), but it will immediately follow *each* time aggression toward siblings occurs.

The behavioral incidents in Table 3 demonstrate the relation between aggression and time-out as well as the lack of time-out for any other misbehaviors.

Note in these six behavioral incidents time-out is implemented only for incidents that constitute the target behavior (i.e., hitting other siblings). It might be tempting for parents to use time-out for some of the other inappropriate behaviors (e.g., demanding of water). However, the parent must accept that time-out cannot be implemented on a whim, but rather is used *every single time* the targeted behavior occurs. In this manner, the child learns that the consequence of that behavior is inevitable; it produces time-out. The decision to add to the list of behaviors producing time-out is done a priori, through careful evaluation of the current plan by the clinician and parents.

Component 2: Specification of Time-Out Length

The length of time the child remains in time-out often varies. In some cases, the child is sent to time-out for 3 minutes and then released. The next time she is released after 30 seconds; the next time after 4 minutes, and so forth. In other cases, the child determines when he gets out of time-out simply by leaving the area when parental supervision is lax. The effective use of time-out requires the clinician and parents to designate a specific minimum length of time in which the child will remain in time-out. This minimum might be extended as a function of the release criteria (to be delineated in the next section). However, the child is required to stay in time-out for the minimum period.

The designated minimum length of time should take into account two factors—the age of the child and the frequency of the behavior. The younger the child, the shorter the time-out interval. For example, in the 1976 study of Porterfield and colleagues, the time-out was less than 1 minute, provided the child was ready to rejoin the activity in an appropriate way. For elementary schoolaged children, the length of time-out might be 1 to 3 minutes. For older children, 3 to 6 minutes might be appropriate.

The second factor to consider in determining the duration of time-out is the frequency of the targeted problem behavior. If the behavior occurs frequently, the time-out duration should be short. The reason becomes fairly obvious with an example: A parent designates a 5-minute minimum duration for time-out. If the child exhibits target behavior 10 times in 30 minutes and the parent implements time-out, the child will probably spend most of his time in time-out. In other words, the child would "live" in time-out. In contrast, a 1- to 2-minute time-out period would allow the child to spend some time in the activity and be praised for any appropriate behavior that may occur.

Component 3: Specification of Designing a Time-Out Area

A place must be designated for the removal of the child contingent on the targeted disruptive behavior. This area should be away from play areas and from other preferable activities or toys. When time-out is ineffective, it is often because parents use a time-out area where the child has ready access to toys or materials (e.g., the child's bedroom as time-out area). While there, the child plays with the toys that are available. Such a time-out loses its effectiveness rapidly. Preventing the child from engaging in play while in time-out makes obvious sense. In everyday usage, however, parents frequently place the child in a time-out area too close to toys or materials. The clinician, must make sure that the parents do not make this mistake.

Component 4: Specification of Release Criteria

Two behavioral requirements need to be addressed with respect to the release criteria: (1) the child stays in time out for a continuous period of time: and (2) the child demonstrates he or she is ready to return to the play activity.

When the child is placed in time-out, it is expected that he or she will remain in that area for the entire time. The child is not allowed to get up and wander around during the time-out period. If the duration of time-out is 2 minutes, the child must remain in the seat for the entire 2 minutes.

The clinician needs to draw the distinction between the right and wrong way of implementing time-out. It is important to teach the parents that 2 minutes of time-out means 2 *continuous* minutes, not 1 minute here, 30 seconds there, 5 seconds here, and 25 seconds there.

Parents can be aided in enforcing a continuous in-seat requirement for time-out by use of the kitchen timer. A kitchen timer is set for the minimum period. If the child gets up before the timer rings the parent places the child back in the time-out chair and resets the timer to the *original* amount of time. The following depicts the contrast between the right and wrong way to implement time-out when the child leaves the seat before the interval is up:

Example 1: Right Way

Child gets up. Parent sits child back down in time-out chair and resets timer to full length of time-out.

Example 2: Wrong Way #1

Child gets up. Child is allowed to rejoin activity: time-out ends.

Example 3: Wrong Way #2

Child gets up. Parent immediately returns child to seat to finish remainder of time.

In example 2, the child learns that when he or she gets up, time-out will end and he or she can rejoin the preferred activity. The child in example 3 learns that the worst that can happen if he or she gets up is being sat back down; the child will learn to get up more frequently to "pass the time" while in time-out.

The child in example 1 learns the right lesson; that is, getting up early results in having to it all over again.

The second requirement is for the child to demonstrate that he or she is ready to rejoin the activity in an appropriate manner at the end of the time-out period. This requirement is called a *time-out compliance set*. In the study of Porterfield and colleagues (1976), this was accomplished by the caregiver's asking the child, "Are you ready to rejoin the activity?" It is important that the child verbally commit to appropriate play and also comply with the parent's request to answer the question. Children who do not comply with the compliance set to leave time-out often engage in the inappropriate behavior again almost immediately. It is important to establish parental control over the child's behavior at this point in the time-out process by getting the child to respond appropriately to the compliance set.

These two requirements for the child's being released from time-out can make the difference between an effective and an ineffective intervention. The following scenario illustrates a consultation incorporating these two requirements.

Mrs. B. is concerned about her two sons (aged 7 and 5), who display disruptive behavior during play activities in the backyard. She meets with Mr. C., a clinician, to discuss this and how time-out might be used. They jointly specify that the following disruptive behaviors will result in time-out: (1) refusal to stop a behavior on command, (2) hitting or fighting with each other, (3) kicking the dog, and (4) throwing a ball against the wall of the house. In the case of hitting or fighting with each other, both boys will be placed in time-out. Mrs. B. will physically take her sons to time-out for each occurrence of any of the targeted behaviors after informing them about what misbehavior produced the time-out (e.g., "You kicked the dog, now you must go sit in time-out and not play").

Mrs. B. and Mr. C. decide that each occurrence of a targeted disruptive behavior will result in a 2-minute time-out for the offender in a chair to the side of the backyard within her view. Mrs. B. removes all toys and other items from this area. She will set the kitchen timers in that area. When the child is escorted to the time-out chair, the kitchen timer will be set for 2 minutes. If the child gets up before the 2-minute period elapses, Mrs. B. will immediately place the boy back in the chair and reset the timer for 2 minutes.

Once the timer indicates that the time-out duration has elapsed, Mrs. B. initiates the compliance set. She goes to the boy and asks the following questions: (1) "What should you not do if you want to stay out of the time out chair?" (2) "Are you sorry you did _____ [behavior]?" and (3) "Are you ready to play nicely?" If the child answers correctly, in a respectful tone, she tells him he can go back and play. If he becomes noncompliant at any point during these questions, she tells him to go back to the time-out chair (and physically helps him to it if necessary), where he will sit and decide if he wants to come back to play. He will sit there for another 30 seconds and then Mrs. B. will initiate the compliance set again. If the child responds appropriately this time to the compliance set, he can then play. If not, the same process is initiated again.

After 6 days of implementing time-out, the rates of disruptive behavior have dropped. Table 2 shows the rates of the targeted disruptive behaviors during the 5 days of baseline data collection and the

Table 2. Data on rates of disruptive behavior for each of Mrs. B.'s sons

	Baseline					Time-Out					
Days	1	2	3	4	5	1	2	3	4	5	6
Child 1	14	16	21	11	13	16	18	9	5	6	3
Child 2	21	15	10	20	15	12	9	3	4	2	4

first 6 days of time-out. Low rates are achieved by the fourth, fifth, and sixth days using time-out.

Component 5: Catching the Child Being Good

The last component of an effective time-out deals with what should happen to the child when he or she re-enters the activity or "time-in" environment. The parents should be taught to praise appropriates and desirable behavior heavily once the child re-enters the activity. Praise can be very effective, particularly when it occurs after the child has received time-out for a targeted disruptive behavior. The child will often seek ways to gain the approval and attention of the parent. Parents must not miss this opportunity!

Once the child is released from time-out, parents should praise (heavily) the following behaviors as soon as they occur:

1. Appropriate isolated play for a short time
2. Appropriate cooperative play for a short time
3. Initiation to play cooperatively
4. Sharing a toy with another child
5. Compliance with requests

The written program in Table 4 illustrates the use of time-out and praise for two disruptive misbehaviors (screaming and running out the door) in a 5-year-old girl in a child care setting.

In this program, Sarah is put in time-out if she screams, throws a tantrum, falls to the floor, or runs out the door unauthorized. She must stay in the time-out seat in the corner for 2 consecutive minutes. Getting up before the kitchen timer rings results in her being put back immediately in time-out with the timer reset to the full 2 minutes. She must be quiet for the last 30 seconds of time-out, which may extend her time. Finally, she must apologize to the caregiver for misbehavior before being

---

Table 4.   Time-out program in child care

---

1. Child's Name: <u>Sarah H.</u>
2. Age: <u>5</u>
3. Parents: <u>Mr. and Mrs. H</u>
4. Time/setting time-out is to be implemented: <u>day care center</u>
5. Types of misbehaviors to result in time-out:
   a. Screaming, tantrums, falling to the floor
   b. running out the door (unauthorized leaving of area)
6. Contingency:
   Each time <u>Sarah</u> (child's name) engages in the above misbehavior(s) _____
   (see examples of above), caregiver will immediately place <u>Sarah</u> (child's name)
   in time-out.
7. Length of time-out: <u>2 minutes (monitored by kitchen timer)</u>
8. Designated time-out area: <u>corner with chair</u>
9. Criteria for release:
   a. Must be in seat for the entire 2 minutes
   b. Must be quiet for the last 30 seconds
   c. Must apologize to caregiver before being allowed to go play
10. After time-out, praise:
   a. First several occurrences of playing nicely with another child
   b. Sharing a toy with another child

---

released from time-out. The caregivers will use heavy praise when Sarah
engages in appropriate behavior on being released from time-out.

☐   What-If Questions for Parents

Questions

1. What if your child gets out of the time-out seat?
2. What if he or she screams while in time-out?
3. What if he or she apologizes while in time-out and then asks to get
   out then?
4. What if your child gets out of the time-out seat and then refuses to
   go back to it?
5. What if your child begins to play with a toy nearby while in time-out?

Answers

1. He or she is immediately put back into the time-out seat (physically
   if necessary), and the timer is reset to the full interval length.

2. If he or she does not get out of the chair, the time-out proceeds. If the child continues to scream during the compliance set, he or she is placed back into time-out for a shorter period and the compliance set is issued again. Compliance must occur without any disruptive behaviors.
3. He or she remains in time-out. Parent should avoid conversation with the child during time-out.
4. He or she is immediately physically guided back to time-out seat or area, and the timer is reset.
5. The toy is taken away immediately, and all toys or objects are removed from the time-out area so that the child would have to get out of the time-out seat to get them, in which case the criteria for getting out of the time-out seat before the interval elapses are put into place.

☐ Summary

Time-out is an effective technique when it is implemented properly and under clinically appropriate conditions. This chapter explains the correct use of this technique for disruptive behaviors of children. The clinician needs to monitor the implementation of the time-out program by parents to enhance the chance for success. Despite rhetoric to the contrary, time-out is an effective "oldy but goody" technique to handle child disruptive behaviors.

III

ADVICE PACKAGES FOR PROBLEM AREAS

CHAPTER

Shopping Trips Can Be Pleasant

Shopping trips are a source of concern for many parents. Having to shop for groceries while managing a child in the store causes anxiety in a lot of families. A Hypothetical illustration of a client's presentation of the problem to the clinician, follows.

> Last Saturday, I took my two children to the grocery store for our weekly shopping trip. When we got there, my older child began running up and down the aisles, grabbing cookies, candy, and potato chips off the shelves and throwing them in the shopping cart. As fast as I could put them back on the shelf, he loaded the cart with three more sets of goodies. When I placed the creme-filled cookies back on the shelf, my toddler (who was in the shopping cart) began to scream. Shoppers glared at us as my toddler could be heard throughout the supermarket. I was embarrassed and humiliated!

For clients in circumstances similar to this illustration, it might be worthwhile to prescribe a specific intervention geared for family shopping trips. Parents can be taught a systematic approach for dealing with child behavior problems during shopping trips, even if their problems are not as severe as in the example.

Determining the need for intervention involves a process of collecting information, evaluating the information, reviewing it with the parents and coming to a consensus with them about the need for intervention

Table 1.   Parent questionnaire: Shopping trips

_____ 1. Does your child wander off to other parts of the store while you are shopping?

_____ 2. Does your child repeatedly call out to you?

_____ 3. Does your child ask or beg you to buy items that are not on the shopping list?

_____ 4. Does your child display poor public manners during shopping trips?

_____ 5. Does your child argue or fight with siblings during shopping trips?

_____ 6. Does your child play tag or other roughhouse games while in the store?

_____ 7. Does your child touch merchandise on the shelves or in the display cases?

_____ 8. Does your child scream or cry excessively during shopping trips?

_____ 9. Do you dread taking your child on a shopping trip?

_____10. Are there behaviors that occur that have not been listed above? If so, specify:

_____

_____

_____

during shopping trips. A first step in this process is to collect information on the parents' perception of the child's behavior during such outings.

The clinician can present parents with the questions in Table 1 to determine whether specific help is needed. Parents indicate for each item whether the behavior happens frequently (F), occasionally (O), or not at all (N). If there is more than one child, the parents should fill out separate questionnaires for each child.

There is no formal scoring of this questionnaire. The questionnaire is reviewed with the parents so that agreement can be reached about whether there is a need for systematic intervention. Some parents think that a few _O_ responses indicate major problems. Others may feel that having several _F_ responses is no cause for concern. Because there are no firm rules, the clinician has to use good clinical judgment to determine whether the reported information indicates that intervention should be recommended.

☐ Questions and Issues About Child Behavior During Shopping Trips

The clinician may need to deal with a number of issues and questions raised by the parents in discussing the need for systematic intervention. The parents may ask whether disruptive behavior is normal or unacceptable and, if the behavior is unacceptable, what kind of discipline system would be effective. Some of these possible questions from parents are here.

Question 1: Are these inappropriate behaviors normal for young children during shopping trips?

This question does not usually need a yes or no answer. Rather, the parents must be made to understand that shopping trips can bring out inappropriate behaviors in many children; that is, such behaviors can occur, but the normality issue is avoided. The clinician can also point out that there are usually two agendas in a shopping trip that can contribute to the potential for problem behavior: The parent wants to get the shopping done as quickly as possible (parent's agenda). At the same time, the supermarket presents a carnival of attractions to bored youngsters. They are not concerned with getting the groceries, but rather are curious about the wrapped packages and goodies. These two agendas sometimes collide, resulting in conflicts between parents and child. Parents should be assured that managing child behavior during shopping trips is a problem experienced by many families, but it does not imply that the child is in need of a psychiatric diagnosis (in most cases) or is not "normal."

Question 2: Do I need to consider obtaining help to intervene in this area?

While many families experience problems during shopping trips, the frequency, intensity, and type of problem behaviors determine whether a family should implement a more systematic approach to managing child behavior during shopping trips.

The clinician should review the parents' answers to the questionnaire to assess the need for intervention with a given family. If *F* responses are given to many of the items, or additional comments representing unacceptable behaviors are provided, the parents may want to implement a systematic package program for shopping trips. They should be concerned, but help is available. And such help is something with which they can be directly involved.

Question 3: Why hasn't what we've tried already worked?

Many children display problem behaviors during shopping trips because of the nature of the situation. Shopping trips occur relatively infrequently and provide a plethora of stimulating objects and situations for children. Therefore, despite the possibility that the child may be reasonably well behaved in other situations as a result of the parental discipline policy, shopping trips may set the occasion for problem behaviors that are otherwise rare.

Therefore, simple solutions or existing discipline strategies may not be the answer. Parents may report that they have tried numerous strategies to control the situation. Such approaches often fail because of the unsystematic nature in which they are tried. This point is important because the advice package may have some components that the parents have tried previously. It is therefore important for the clinician to emphasize that the advice package he or she is suggesting is more comprehensive than a few techniques and requires *systematic* implementation. In addition, parents should be told that tactics such as coercion, scolding, and pleading usually do not lead to overall long-term changes in a child's behavior and that such tactics will not be part of the systematic advice package. What is required in many cases is a comprehensive package approach that addresses the problem behaviors in a proactive manner. The next section presents an empirical basis for an advice package for shopping trips.

☐ Brief Description

The family advice package for shopping trips involves teaching the parents to develop guidelines for acceptable child behavior during shopping trips and to provide monetary consequences for appropriate and inappropriate behavior. The parents are taught to systematically enforce the guidelines by removing money or points for each infraction of the guidelines. In addition, they are taught to engage the children in the shopping experience while keeping the trip short initially to promote success.

☐ Empirical Basis for the Advice Package

It is surprising that although problems on shopping trips have been prevalent in American families throughout our history (or at least with the development of grocery stores and supermarkets), a child management strategy specifically designed for this setting was nonexistent until the mid-1970s. Problems during shopping trips, and families in need of help, were at that time brought to the attention of a group of child psychologists at the University of Kansas (Clark, Greene, MacRae, McNees, Davis, & Risley, 1977). They became interested in devising a comprehensive package program for parents who face this ordeal. These researchers began by surveying adult shoppers (with and without children) and store personnel to determine what kinds of problems were encountered during shopping trips. The respondents of the survey listed 112 behavior problems. They indicated that severely disruptive youngsters antagonized not only their parents but other shoppers and store personnel as well. These results indicated to the researchers that parents needed a strategy that worked in this arena. The child psychologists began to devise a program to solve problem behaviors during shopping trips for two families who volunteered for the study. Each family had three children, two boys and one girl, ranging from 7 to 11 years old.

During the study, the parents were instructed to shop in two different stores for a 16-minute period, which is fairly short in comparison with more usual shopping trips. During each shopping trip, observers from the university watched the children and recorded disruptive child behavior in two categories: distracting comments, and distracting behaviors. After collecting some initial data on the rates of these behaviors during the baseline condition, the child psychologists developed a comprehensive program they called a "shopping trip advice package." The major components of this advice package were the development of specific child behavior guidelines and the enforcement of these guidelines through monetary consequences. The two families were taught how to implement this advice package by graduate students at the University of Kansas.

Specific guidelines were set up to differentiate acceptable from unacceptable behavior. The children were told by their parents that they could each have a stipend of 50 cents after the trip if they followed the new courteous behavior rules for shopping. The specifics of each guideline were reviewed by the parents with their children. The children were also told that if their behavior was disturbing o annoying (i.e., violated a rule), they would be fined 5 cents in each instance and be told exactly what rule had been broken.

Once the parents were trained in setting and enforcing these child behavior guidelines, they found a dramatic reduction in distracting comments and disruptive behavior following just a few deductions in the child's 50-cent stipend. Only once did one of the children lose all the stipend as a result of repeated fines during a single shopping excursion. Could a strategy work for shopping trips? The answer for these two families was a resounding *yes*.

The parents were given a questionnaire after the study to determine whether they liked the program and whether they believed that it had made a difference in their child's behavior. Both sets of parents indicated that the advice package definitely improved the shopping trips with their children and created a much more pleasant situation (for both them and their children). The parents particularly noted their relief at being able to stop issuing ineffective warnings, similar to the following we have all heard at one time or another: "Behave or else!" "Don't touch that toy!" "I'm warning you for the last time." With a strict enforcement of the guidelines and consequences for disruptive behavior, the need for coercive comments to attempt to gain control of the child's behavior diminished. The advice package also provided an educational experience for the children. Instead of being disruptive, the youngsters were now active participants in the shopping trip.

Finally, the 50-cent stipend did not seem to add to the shopping budget significantly. When the parents compared this amount with what they were spending previously to keep their children quiet, they saw that the previous costs exceeded the current stipend.

☐ Components of the Advice Package

There are two basic components in the design of an advice package for parents to use during shopping trips:

1. Development of acceptable child behavior guidelines or rules
2. Establishment of consequences for violation of guidelines and rules and of rewards for nonviolation of such guidelines and rules

Component 1: Development of Acceptable Guidelines for Child Behavior

Establishing child behavior guidelines for acceptable shopping behavior is a necessity for both the parent and the children. Guidelines let each party realize their responsibilities. Without specific guidelines, parents tend to be both vague and fluctuating in their demands, criticism, and acceptance of child behavior, often within the span of a few minutes. Youngsters are then forced to interpret such fluctuations, with unsatisfactory results for all concerned.

For example, what does a parent actually mean when he or she says "behave." Does this mean the child should, can or cannot touch a given toy? Suppose the child only walks up to the toy but does not touch it? Is that permissible? Not spelling out what is acceptable and unacceptable leaves the judgment open to interpretation. What the child interprets as acceptable, may not be acceptable to the parents. Guidelines provide more concrete criteria for acceptable behavior.

Table 2.   Guidelines for acceptable child behavior

1. *Stay close to the shopping cart or parents.*
   The child should be within arm's reach of the parent, the shopping cart, or a sibling who is touching the cart.
2. *Make no distracting remarks.*
   The child should not argue with the parents or siblings, tease siblings, or repeatedly call out to either. He or she should not beg, ask, or demand that the parents buy something not on the shopping list or request to go into another section of the store.
3. *Display good manners.*
   Yelling, fighting, roughhousing, hanging all over the cart, playing tag, playing other games, and excessive whining or crying are not permitted.
4. *Do not touch the store merchandise.*
   The child should not pick up any of the items on the shelves, display cases, or aisle displays.

Table 2 contains child behavior guidelines taken from the study described earlier (Clark et al, 1977) and recommended for adoption in implementing the advice package.

Once the clinician has delineated these general guidelines for the parents, he or she should present specifics to teach them examples of violations of each rule. Each guideline should be discussed separately with the parents. Scenarios depicting a child's behavior can be presented and the parents asked whether a guideline was violated. This exercise allows the clinician to teach the parents the specific circumstances under which a guideline is violated. Two possible examples follow:

Example 1

Therapist: "Let's go over the guideline involving staying close to the shopping cart or to you. Suppose your child wanders away from you and then says, 'Oops, I forgot. I was supposed to stay close to you. I'm sorry. It won't happen again.' Was this rule [guideline] violated?"

The answer is yes. Apologizing for the violation does not erase the occurrence of the behavior.

Example 2

Therapist: "Suppose your son says to your daughter, 'You're fat!' After you point out this violation, he denies having said it. Did a rule violation occur?"
The answer is yes. One does not need to produce witnesses to attest to the validity of a finding. The parent is the judge and the jury. Also, arguing with the parent continues to violate guideline 2.

Table 3.   Contingency contract

Behavior		Consequence
When child follows the guidelines	→	Stipend is earned (50 cents possible per trip).
When child does not follow the guidelines	→	Fine is 5 cents for each infraction.

Component 2: Developing Consequences for Behavior

Just designing guidelines for acceptable behavior is not an answer in and of itself. It is important to provide consequences for acceptable behavior (i.e., following guidelines) and consequences for unacceptable behavior (i.e., violating guidelines). In this advice package, consequences are set up with a stipend and response cost method.

Depending on the age of the child, the parents might draw up a written contract to provide him or her with a clear specification of what is acceptable and what is not acceptable and the consequences for both. For younger children, the agreement may be oral. Table 3 contains an example of the contingency contract using the 50-cent stipend method.

Before specifying the contingencies to be implemented, the parents should collect baseline data during the next few shopping trips. This can be done by using the shopping stipend card in Table 4, which tracks the occurrence of each rule violation. In this contract, the child begins with 50 cents. He had two infractions of not staying close to the cart, one distracting remark, and no occurrences, of bad manners or touching merchandise. Each time an infraction of one of the guidelines occurs, 5 cents

Table 4.   Shopping stipend card

Rule Violation	Frequency									
Not close to cart	①	②	3	4	5	6	7	8	9	10
Distracting remarks	①	2	3	4	5	6	7	8	9	10
Bad manners	1	2	3	4	5	6	7	8	9	10
Touching merchandise	1	2	3	4	5	6	7	8	9	10

is deducted from the child's stipend. In this particular case, 15 cents would have been subtracted from the 50-cent stipend.

Parents should be taught that the fine must be consistent, automatic, and without exception. They do not need to scream, yell, or holler at the child while levying the fine. Rather, in a neutral tone, they should indicate the behavior that is unacceptable and the levying of the fine. Here is a hypothetical dialogue between a mother and her son, Billy, during a shopping trip:

Mother: Well, I see the next thing on my shopping list is bread. Do you know where we can find the bread?

Billy: I want Brand X cookies, Mom. Bobby's mother buys them for him.

Mother: It is distracting when you ask for items not on my list. You broke the rule about this. I'll have to take 5 cents from your 50-cent allowance.

Billy: That's no fair! Bobby's mother buys Brand X cookies.

Mother: That's another distracting remark. I'll have to deduct another 5 cents. Now let's go find the bread. What aisle do you think it would be in?

Billy: Aisle 7. I saw it on the billboard in the front of the store wall.

Mother: Why, thank you! It's so nice to have you around to help me.

In this scenario, a fine was levied each time an infraction occurred. The levying of the fine occurred immediately after the rule violation and was short, sweet, and to the point. The mother did not scream at her son. Finally, she immediately reinforced appropriate behavior when it occurred (see last interchange).

The following is another dialogue that might occur with a different guideline violation.

Sue: picks up a bottle of hair shampoo and attempts to unscrew its cap:

Father: taking shampoo out of the child's hands and placing it back on the shelf): "Sue, you're not supposed to touch any of the items on the shelf. I'm withholding 5 cents of your stipend.

Sue: I'm sorry. I forgot.

Father: Okay. Let's try to remember the rule. Now what's next on our list?

Sue: Can I get the nickel back? I said I'm sorry.

Father: Sue, you broke a rule, and you have to be fined. Also, you're now distracting me from shopping, so I'll have to withhold another 5 cents [marks infraction on shopping list]. What would you guess we're having for dinner tonight?

Sue: Spaghetti? I like spaghetti with meatballs.

Father: I know you do. How was school yesterday? Did you do well in reading? *[Parent continues to another aisle with child.]*

The clinician should point out to the parents that apologies from the child do not mean that the fine is removed. They should acknowledge the child's apology but indicate that he or she has to live with the *consequences* of the behavior.

☐ Additional Components of the Advice Package

Two additional components of the package shopping trip advice enhance its effectiveness.

Component 1: Engaging the child during the shopping trip

Can parents use the shopping trip to spend quality time with children? Of course, the answer is yes. In a proactive approach, parents should not only determine what the child should not be doing but also provide alternative opportunities. Children should not be yelling, screaming, and playing tag in the supermarket. But what should they be doing while their parents are shopping? If a child has nothing to do, he or she will become bored. It is unreasonable to expect a child to just tag along and not become involved in the activity. What is often overlooked is that the shopping trip can be an educational experience for the child, with the parent as the teacher. The grocery store offers vast opportunities for children to practice skills that they learn in school, such as reading, number identification, math, use of money, and possibly learning how to develop a family budget.

To use the store as a classroom, parents must consider the child's age in relation to what is expected of him or her. The parents can keep the child's attention by making him or her a meaningful, useful part of the trip. The following dialogue between a parent and a 6-year-old girl illustrates how a mother can transform the shopping trip into a learning experience:

Mother: Okay, Mary, next on our list is soup. Where do you think we might find that? *[The mother engages her daughter.]*

Mary: I don't know.

Mother: Well, we can look for it on the signs that are posted in the middle of each aisle. But I'll bet we can find it next to the other canned goods.

Mary: Let's go across each aisle and look at the signs. *[Mary helps move the shopping cart.]*

Mother: Mary, what's the difference between making chicken soup from the can and making it from scratch?

Mary: It's easier to make soup from the can. You just heat it up and then eat it.

Mother: That's right. Homemade chicken soup takes a lot more time. You have to cook the chicken, make the broth, and add the noodles. You know, I really enjoy shopping with you when you are helpful and pleasant. *[The mother reinforces good behavior.]*

This interactive approach requires effort on the part of the parents, especially in the beginning, when they may run out of subjects to discuss with the child. However, as parents gain more practice at this type of interaction, they will become more relaxed and comfortable with it. For the first few shopping trips, parents may report fatigue caused by the increased child/parent interaction, and this is to be expected.

Another sample dialogue with Mary and her mother demonstrates how basic reading and math skills can be augmented during shopping:

Mary: Mom, here's the soup. Which kind do you want?

Mother: Well, let's see. It looks like there are several companies that produce canned chicken soup. Can you tell me who these companies are by reading the labels?

Mary: This one says Brand X and that one says Brand Y. On the label it says they're both chicken soup.

Mother: Right! Now let's look and see how much each one costs. Both are 10 ounces. What does that mean?

Mary: I don't know.

Mother: If both are 10 ounces, we know there is the same amount of soup concentrate in each can. But Brand X is marked 28 cents and Brand Y is marked 47 cents. Which one costs less?

Mary: I think Brand X.

Mother: Very good. Since we want the one that costs less, can you get it for me and put it in the shopping cart?

Mary: Will I lose a nickel for touching?

Mother: No, because I told you to get it for me. You lose a nickel when you touch merchandise that I haven't told you to get for me. But that's a really good question. I'm glad to see you're on your toes in obeying the guidelines. Now, can you help me find the tomato soup?

Mary: It's right here! And there are four different kinds.

Mother: That's a little harder, but let's see if you can help me again in picking out the brand that costs the least.

Component 2: Taking Shorter Trips in the Beginning of the Program

Even if parents are using all the suggestions given so far, the child may still have a hard time behaving acceptably for a long shopping trip. Parents must realize that the child will need some time to get used to behaving in an acceptable fashion for an entire length of a normal shopping trip. Parents should initially stack the cards in their favor (and their child's favor) by reducing the length of the trip and thereby taking more frequent trips.

For example, if a shopping trip usually lasts about 45 minutes, the parents can take two or three 20-minute trips. Each trip will give the child practice in learning how to behave. The shortened length of the trip also promotes the possibility that the child will earn most or all of the stipend. With improvements in child behavior, the trips can gradually be made longer, as shown in Table 5.

☐ Possible Questions About the Advice Package

Once the advice package has been explained to parents questions might arise. Here are a few possible questions and suggestions for how to handle them.

Question 1: Doesn't this advice package amount to bribery?

The use of the stipend and the subsequent fines teaches the child that appropriate behavior is rewarded and inappropriate behavior has consequences. The parents are not bribing their child because there is a difference between bribes and a systematic incentive program for appropriate

Table 5.   Progressive increases in trip duration.

	Number of Trips	Duration
Phase I	5	10–15 minutes
Phase II	4	15–25 minutes
Phase III	3	25–45 minutes
Phase IV	2	45–50 minutes

behavior. The clinician must indicate to the parents that bribes are more along the lines of random, inconsistent offers of incentives. The advice package provides a designated reward system for appropriate behavior. Also, bribes are often used by parents after the child behaved unacceptably. With the incentive program, the child knows that good behavior results in rewards and in inappropriate behavior results in the loss of such. The presentation of consequences for behavior imparts an important reality of life to a child.

Question 2: Is it necessary to be consistent?

Some parents may find rigid adherence to the monetary fine contingency to be unduly strict. Often, it is inconsistent application that has failed in the past. The parents need to be taught that consistency in implementing the consequences for acceptable and unacceptable behavior eventually teaches the child to behave appropriately during shopping trips. Irregular enforcement serves only to demonstrate to the child that behavior during one period of time will not be treated in the same fashion as the same behavior at another time. Parents *must* follow through with the planned consequences of each occurrence of behavior.

Question 3: How much of a fine should there be?

Stipend amounts and fine rates per violation can differ depending on the age of the child and the parents' resources. Whatever stipend amount is designated, the fine should be small in proportion to the potential stipend. If the parents have collected baseline data, the clinician and parents can determine how many fines might occur on the first couple of trips. With this information, the fine amount is adjusted so that with just a minimal improvement above baseline, the child can earn a fair proportion of the stipend.

The value of the fine and the stipend can be adjusted as the child begins to improve. The fine amounts can be slightly increased or the stipend amount increased once the child reduces the number of instances of rule violations.

Question 4: Should I allow the child to spend all of the stipend in the next trip?

Earned stipend amounts can be spent on the next shopping trip to purchase a preferred item, or they can be accumulated to buy something more expensive. This flexibility teaches the child to develop appropriate shopping behaviors. One stipulation about any spending policy that is developed, however, is that the child may not spend any of his or her previous savings during a shopping trip in which less than half of the full stipend was earned. For example, if the stipend was 50 cents with a 5-cent fine, at least 25 cents would have to be earned on the current shopping trip in order to spend money accrued on the next trip. This allows parents to teach the child that if a horrible shopping trip occurs, he or she will have to wait longer (an additional week, possibly) to spend the money.

Question 5: How does one keep track of the fines?

Keeping track of the fines in one's head during shopping trips is asking for trouble. A written record is needed. Table 6 shows how parents can keep track of the fines while keeping an eye on the shopping list. Each time a fine is levied, the parents circle the next fine amount. In this case, Mary was fined once and Bobby twice.

If the shopping list illustration in Table 6 is not feasible, parents can also use golf counters or other methods to keep track of the fines. The method is not as important as the accuracy of the fine-tracking system. It is also important that parents bring in their data to therapy sessions so the clinician can review both quantitative data (number of fines) and subjective data (e.g., how do parents think the advice package is working?). Table 7 is a summary sheet with hypothetical data that parents might fill out before a session for review by the clinician.

Question 6: Should we review the behavior guidelines before each trip?

If the children have questions about specific aspects of the guidelines, it would be helpful to review them before being in the grocery store. Once

Table 6.   Sample shopping list for a parent with two children

| | Fines | |
Shopping Items	Mary	Bobby
Ice cream	5 cents	15 cents
Bread	5 cents	15 cents
Margarine	5 cents	15 cents
Carrots	5 cents	15 cents
Lettuce	5 cents	15 cents
Milk	5 cents	15 cents

Table 7.   Summary data sheet for shopping trips

Date	Trip	Length	Child	Number of Fines	Number of Fines Possible
6/21	Store X	15 minutes	Bobby	2	10
			Susan	1	10
6/23	Store Z	20 minutes	Bobby	1	10
			Susan	3	10

the children are in the grocery store, the enforcement of the guidelines should be straightforward and the fines levied consistently.

Question 7: Can preschoolers benefit from this approach?

These methods were found to be successful with children between the ages of 4 and 10 in the previous research, but what can be done for parents who have children younger than 4? With young children, certain aspects of this plan would have to be altered to suit their level of under-standing. A suggested first change would be to enforce one guideline at a time. For example, the young child may initially be responsible only for staying close to the cart. After the child has demonstrated weeks of obedience to this guideline, another guideline can be explained and enforced, such as not touching store merchandise. Adding one guideline at a time allows the preschool child to understand what is presented and to respond appropriately. Only when the child demonstrates capability of following one targeted guideline should another be presented for enforcement.

A second modification might concern the reward and fining method. Instead of money, stickers or other visual displays on a board can be used. The enforcement procedure would remain the same. At the point at which a fine occurs for violating a rule, a sticker might be removed from the child's chart. A line should be drawn through the chart to illustrate at what point the child does or does not earn a specific reward. Finally, the child should be given the reward at the end of the shopping trip, rather than the following week. Young children need more immediate access to reinforcement than do older children. As with older children, however, the parents must state the guideline or guidelines clearly and check for misunderstanding by asking questions about what is acceptable and unacceptable behavior. They must use simple words and, if possible, act out (role play, pantomime) the acceptable behaviors while at home.

Question 8: Will this program work for everyone?

No program works for every situation and every family. Although the described plan for dealing with the shopping trip dilemma was designed from a research study that demonstrated success, it is highly conceivable that the strategy might have to be altered in some cases for successful results. The clinician might consider keeping the general method intact and altering such things as the allowance amount, the amount of time spent in the store, and whether both parents go along to help implement the plan.

In summary, the following steps can be used to implement this advice package with parents:

1. Develop guidelines and rules for acceptable child behavior.
2. Set consequences (stipends) for following guidelines.
3. Set consequences (fines) for violations of guidelines.
4. Inform the child of the system and give examples of violations.
5. Develop a tracking system.
6. Initially keep shopping trips shorter, but more frequent, than usual.
7. Engage the child actively in shopping.
8. Implement the system during each trip.
9. Pay the stipend at the end of the trip and allow the child to spend the stipend on a future trip.

☐ Summary

Shopping trips do not have to be something parents dread. By using an advice package that identifies specific misbehaviors and removes a certain amount of a stipend for each misbehavior (rule violation), parents can help children learn to behave more appropriately during shopping trips. Additionally, they can use the shopping trip to teach a variety of other valuable skills, so that the grocery store becomes a "learning lab" for children.

An Advice Package for Dining Out at Family Restaurants

☐ Presenting Problem

Imagine you and your spouse are going out for dinner. You've selected a wonderful restaurant with great food, great atmosphere, and great service. Are you beginning to feel relaxed and ecstatic about the evening and enjoyable conversation with your spouse? Oops, did I forget to mention that your four kids will be accompanying you? Will the dining experience sound something like this?

> "Johnny, quit banging the table with the spoon. It's not to be used as a drumstick."
> "Sarah, you're supposed to *sit on* the chair, not lie under it."
> "Frank, get back to the table and sit like a normal person."
> "Sarah, stop teasing your sister" (as the sister cries and sobs). "See, now you made her cry. This is supposed to be a happy time for all of us."
> "Oh, why do we bother? It's easier to stay home."

In many families dining out is a challenging experience rather than a rewarding one. Many families redesign their dining experience to revolve around the children's needs and behavior, in stark contrast to their dining plans and experiences before they had children. Some parents eschew dining out excursions altogether to avoid situations that arise in restaurants. It is certainly an area that can warrant attention from a clinical standpoint.

What makes the dining experience in a family restaurant a problem situation? Children who normally do not misbehave can exhibit unacceptable behaviors during family dining experiences (Baumann, Reiss, Rogers, and Bailey, 1983). The nature of restaurants may be the source of the problems. Family restaurants may render traditional consequences (such as time-out) unfeasible, thereby rendering parents ineffective at managing inappropriate child behaviors.

To determine whether a family is in need of a systematic plan for dining out excursions, a few questions for parents on their experiences with their children are helpful. The questions in Table 1 can be used to evaluate the family's current distress level subjectively. The data generated from these questions are used to get a brief glimpse of the family's current level of distress during restaurant outings, the types of problems encountered, and other information relevant to this setting. If the parents indicate that the child's behavior is a problem, their response to the second question in section III can be used to determine whether dining out is a specific situation that causes problems or is just reflective of a lack of parental control over the child's behavior under a variety of everyday circumstances. If the dining experience is a unique source of concern to the parents, this advice package is well suited. If the dining experience is reflective of a more general state of problem behavior, the clinician must determine whether intervention should begin with this situation or whether other more serious situations warrant immediate attention.

☐ Questions and Issues About Child Behavior During Dining Out

The clinician may need to deal with a number of questions and issues raised by parents about their child's behavior during restaurant outings. Some possible questions and answers follow.

Question 1: Why is my child such a problem when we're dining out? He isn't usually so unmanageable.

What parents consider a pleasurable and relaxing dining experience typically involves conditions under which many children get bored. Dining

Table 1.   Parent questionnaire: Dining out

Section I. Distress Level
Rate the following questions on a 1 to 9 scale using the anchor points below:

	1	3	7	9
	Never	Seldom	Often	Always

_____	Do you have to remind your child to behave appropriately while in a restaurant?
_____	Does your child behave in a manner that embarrasses you?
_____	Do you postpone or avoid going out to eat primarily for reasons involving your child's behavior in the restaurant?
_____	Do you feel as if there is nothing you can do to control the situation?

Section II—Types of Problem
The following questions can be used to get an idea of the types of problem behaviors parents encounter during dining excursions. Next to each item, indicate whether the behavior never occurs (N), occurs on some trips but not all (S), occurs every trip (E), or occurs multiple times during each trip (MT)

_____	Plays with utensils, napkins, glasses
_____	Leaves table without permission
_____	Argues or fights with sibling(s)
_____	Argues or fights with parent(s)
_____	Throws tantrums
_____	Throws food

Section III—General Information
1. What strategies have you used to get your child to behave more appropriately during restaurant outings?
2. Are the problems displayed during restaurant outings typical or atypical of the child's behavior? In other words, do you have problems with the child's behavior just during restaurant outings, or are there other times or places where inappropriate or disruptive behavior is problem?
3. Do you have any other comments that have not been covered by previous questions?

out is supposed to allow adults *to relax* and not worry about cooking, dinner preparation, clean-up, and so forth. The parents' agenda while dining out is to have a relaxing, quiet evening. However, just relaxing is not an activity many children want to engage in for long periods (in some cases, 10 seconds is too long). Children usually want to be doing something. Their agenda involves movement and engaging in new experiences. With these two different agendas comes conflict. If the child cannot find something appropriate to be entertained with or by, he or she is likely to resort to something inappropriate. Therefore, otherwise, reasonably behaved children can be problems while in restaurants.

Question 2: Should we avoid going out to restaurants until my child gets older?

Of course, this is a decision for the family. However, if the enjoy going out to restaurants, the advice package presented later can be offered as a means to an end. It offers them hope that they may not have to forgo the pleasurable event of eating out until their children grow up. In the interim, the parents can be encouraged to dine out without their children (by getting a babysitter) so as to enjoy themselves without the hassles of dealing with child behaviors.

Question 3: Time-out works in the home, but it doesn't seem to work in restaurants. How come?

Time-out might be a logical, effective consequence for inappropriate behaviors in a restaurant. However, its application can be logistically difficult, if not impossible, in this setting. Where does one isolate the child when the parents remove him or her for being disruptive in the restaurant? To a chair away from the table? Even if one were to do so, would such a procedure invoke an escalation of the behavior? If so, how would the parents deal with such an escalation? Additionally, if time-out were used, is it practical to implement 5, 10, or 15 times at a given meal? Implementation of time-out is not just logistically tough but can also be extremely aversive for the parents to do in the needed fashion. These factors render time-out difficult and ineffective in restaurants.

Question 4: How about using verbal reminders when the child acts inappropriately? Shouldn't that teach them?

Many parents use verbal reminders, such as "Johnny, remember the rule for not touching the utensils!" Everyone has heard such verbal prompts, reminders, or restatement of rules coming from parents in restaurants. Although common, such reminders are generally ineffective and often lead only to additional louder reminders and prompts. The inability of such traditional child management strategies to immediately evoke appropriate behavior leads many parents to dread family dining out experiences.

Question 5: Can anything be done to bring sanity to family dining experiences?

Given the difficulty of implementing typical consequences for undesirable behavior, what, if any, strategies can be used to ameliorate child behavior problems during dining out experiences? The answer lies in having the parents set up premeal dining experiences that will preempt child misbehavior by promoting appropriate behavior.

☐ Brief Description

The family advice package for restaurant outings involves teaching the parents an effective way to structure the premeal time. It involves rearranging where the family and children sit, removing items likely to lead to inappropriate or disruptive behavior, and engaging children in activities that lessen the chance that they will seek out other ways of entertaining themselves.

☐ An Empirical Basis for the Advice Package

Researchers at Florida State University were interested in developing an advice package for parents who were having difficulty with children who were normally well behaved during family dining outings (Baumann, Reiss, Rogers, & Bailey, 1983). Before developing an advice package, the researchers conducted a survey of parents, which indicated that during family dining out experiences, the premeal time (i.e., the time before the meal is delivered by the server) was deemed to be the most problem-filled part of the excursion. During the meal, fewer problems were reported, since children were kept busy consuming their food. However, the premeal period, which could be 20 minutes or more, would occasion disruptive or inappropriate behaviors from children who were normally well behaved.

With this information, the researchers set about designing an advice package that would address the problem premeal time for families. When they had designed the advice package, they initially tested it with two volunteer families who reported needing help when dining out. A restaurant in the Tallahassee area was contacted, and it agreed to provide the families with a 50% discount on the cost of the dinners to facilitate the implementation of the study. A video camera was used to collect direct observational data on child misbehavior. To make the experience as normal as possible for the participating families, the video camera was screened from the main dining room so that other customers were not aware the family was being videotaped. Because of the logistic and practical concerns, only one child per family, labeled as the most disruptive by the parents, was selected for videotaping and subsequent measurement of inappropriate behaviors.

Four categories of inappropriate behaviors were measured: (1) inappropriate verbal behavior (e.g., crying, whining, interrupting others, demanding things); (2) inappropriate motor behavior (e.g., standing on the chair, being out of chair without permission, hitting or kicking others); (3) inappropriate use of food utensils (e.g., playing with dinner utensils, tossing food into the mouth); and (4) noncompliance (i.e., not complying with a parental request within a certain time).

The advice package was designed to restructure the way in which the families conducted themselves during the premeal time. Events that would engage the child in appropriate behavior were identified and presented during the premeal time such as providing small toys for the child to occupy his or her time. A copy of the package is available from Dr. Ken Baumann of Behavioral Management Consultants in Tallahassee, Florida.

The data were collected during two visits to the restaurant. In the first visit, baseline data were collected on inappropriate behaviors for comparison purposes. Before the second visit to the restaurant, the parents were taught how to implement the advice package. They read the instructional material, and the experimenter answered any questions they had. During the second visit, after a few minutes (for collection of pretreatment data), the parents began using the components in the advice package while data collection continued. Dramatic changes in child behavior followed the implementation of the advice package.

For example, before treatment with the advice package, Family 2 recorded between 30% to 100% inappropriate behavior levels from the targeted child. After implementation of the advice package, the same child demonstrated inappropriate behaviors less than 20% of the time during the outing. That is, the child's worst period during the advice package was far better that his best period during baseline.

In a second related experiment, the same researchers used an additional nine families to test the advice package and found the same dramatic results. Parental compliance with the advice package was fairly high among all families. In general, the advice package took only about 10 minutes to read, which is a minimal investment of time to learn to be effective.

Finally, survey data indicated that seven of the nine families in the second study reported that the package was easy to implement, all nine families reported that it was very helpful in reducing inappropriate child behavior, and eight of nine indicated that they would probably or definitely use the package in the future.

An additional study conducted at Southern Illinois University at Carbondale found a similar result when material that would engage parents and children during dining out was introduced (Green, Hardison, & Greene, 1984). In this study, the researchers developed a unique placemat called Table Talk. They compared the effects of a traditional placemat during dining with those of Table Talk on inappropriate behavior in children. The results indicated that the Table Talk placemats were far more effective in reducing children's distracting comments and disruptive behavior as well as increasing parents' and children's social and educational comments.*

☐ Components of the Family Advice Package

The components of the family advice package offered in this chapter are those described in the study by Baumann and colleagues (1983):

1. Specifying appropriate child behavior for the restaurant.
2. Locating a table or booth away from the crowd
3. Seating the children on the inside, next to the wall
4. Separating the children
5. Providing the children with a premeal snack
6. Ordering food the children enjoy
7. Providing small, interesting toys to occupy their time
8. Moving the dinner utensils from the children's reach during the premeal period
9. Removing the toys when the food arrives
10. Periodically praising the children for appropriate behavior or providing a point system

Component 1: Specifying Appropriate Child Behavior

In describing the appropriate behaviors to the child, the parents can use the standard set of appropriate behaviors listed in Table 2 and revise it as

---

*More information on the Table Talk placemat and its advice program for parents can be obtained from Brandon F. Greene, Ph.D., at the Behavior Analysis and Therapy Program at Southern Illinois University at Carbondale, IL 62901.

Table 2.   Appropriate child behaviors for restaurant

---

1. Talking in an appropriate conversational tone
2. Making a request in an acceptable vocal manner
3. Sitting in the chair
4. Keeping the hands and feet to oneself
5. Using utensils appropriately
6. Eating food appropriately
7. Complying with parental requests

---

needed. To design a list from scratch, the clinician should interview the parents to determine what child problem behaviors occur in the restaurant and to identify what appropriate behaviors should occur in place of the problem behaviors. It might be easier to use the list in Table 2, adding or deleting as a function of parental input.

Component 2 and 3: Locating a Table away From the Crowd and Seat Children Next to the Wall

Finding a table away from the crowd reduces distractions that arise when children are seated near others. Placing the children next to the wall cuts down their opportunities to get out of their seats and wander away. During the beginning part of the intervention, parents can be advised to find restaurants, or times to go dining, in which they can easily meet these two requirements, that is, pick less frequented restaurants or visit at slow times during the day. As the children develop appropriate behaviors and begin to engage in activities during the premeal period, it becomes possible to alter these two conditions gradually. Parents could eventually have the children sit anywhere in the restaurant and not necessarily against the wall. It is not recommended to test the absence of these two components on the first few instances of implemention of the advice package; however.

Component 4: Separating the Children

Many parents have learned that seating children together creates a trouble situation. The fourth component of the advice package involves separating the children, if possible, by having parents sit between them. If this is not possible, space or an additional seat should be placed between the children. Obviously, if there are many children in the family, this becomes less possible at one table or booth. It might be advisable for larger families to get two booths and to divide the older and the younger children so that there are a few older children between the two booths. In that manner, there might be a few older children with a few younger children at one booth (where the mother is) and a few older children and a few younger children in the other booth (where the father is eating). Again, as the children begin to engage in appropriate behavior, the groups can eat at one table by having older children sit between younger children and parents.

An additional requirement that helps reduce inappropriate behavior while the children are in their seats is to (whenever possible) sit at tables rather than in booths. Booths seem to encourage children to wiggle and move about, which often leads to their ducking under the table. With tables, the chair can be pushed in so that ducking under the table becomes a less probable behavior. Additionally, the chair does not allow the latitude of the movement in the seat that a booth does.

Component 5: Providing a Premeal Snack

The premeal snack should be given either right before the meal is served or on appropriate request by the child. Possible premeal snack items include soda crackers, vegetable appetizers, and olives. Before the family gets in the car to go to the restaurant, the children should identify what they would like as a premeal snack, but the snacks should not compete with the consumption of the main meal (e.g., candy, cookies, potato chips). The function of the premeal snack is not to fill the child, but rather to occupy his or her time as well as to take the edge off the child's hunger. It is particularly relevant if the meal is delayed or the child is dining at a time later than he or she normally eats.

The family should also attempt to find restaurants where the food is served within a certain period of time, preferably no more than 20 minutes. A longer wait sets children up for failure. They finish the snack, get bored with the toys, and engage in an undesirable behavior.

Component 6: Ordering Food the Children Enjoy

Ordering food children do not like sets the occasion for argument. The children should be encouraged to make their food selection ahead of time while still at home. Parents might say, "Okay, kids, we're going to restaurant XYZ. You can order from the children's menu, and it has the following choices: Tiny Tiger Pizza, Baby Chicken strips, and Miniburger.

Let's start with Johnny. Johnny, what do you want to eat? *[Johnny chooses]* Susan, what do you want?"

It is important to get the child to choose ahead of time in cases in which misbehavior has occurred previously around the ordering process. The child's choice can be written on a slip of paper, and then the child can hand that to the parent or the server at the appropriate time. As this slight modification of ordering begins to reduce misbehavior during ordering, the child can be allowed to choose while at the restaurant.

Component 7: Providing Interesting Toys

Providing toys for the child to play with before delivery of the meal is a good distraction for him or her. Toys parents might consider for younger children include blocks, legos, coloring books, story books, drawing paper, mazes, and puzzles with letters and numbers.

In the case of toys that involve many pieces, such as Legos, or blocks, only a limited number of pieces should be brought to the restaurant. Having dozens of pieces of Legos spread out at the dining table increases the chances of child movement out of the seat and works against a quick clean-up when the meal comes. If coloring books are used, only a few crayons should be brought. The child can choose five colors before the trip. Books are good items to bring since they provide parents and children with a mutually engaging activity. It is important to involve children in activities with parent participation.

Toys that have had occasioned aggressive play in the child are not recommended. If the child has dolls or play figures that are typically used with a lot of motion while at home (e.g., Power Rangers), such behavior will probably occur if those toys were available during the premeal time. Although moving about with the play figures or crashing them into each other may be acceptable at home, it would not be acceptable at the restaurant were the child to smash the toy into the wall or dip it into a glass of water.

For older children, small games, such as cards, checkers, or chess, are appropriate. For example, Nintendo or Sega Genesis games are entertaining items that can engage the child in an activity and minimizes problem behavior.

If the desire is to involve the whole family, one might bring Trivial Pursuit or another game that has a question and answer format. Again, only a limited portion of the game should be brought so that clean-up time and the possibility of loss of some of the materials are minimized. An excellent game for the entire family is Brain Quest, which contains 1500 questions and answers for various grades and ages. It fits nicely in a pocketbook or carrying case and contains appropriate questions for all ages in the family.

Component 8: Removal of Dinner Utensils During the Premeal Period

Playing with the spoon, fork, knife, napkins, cups, or glasses seems to be a universal problem for young children. If the family adopts premeal activities that are advocated in this advice package, playing with dinner utensils should be less appealing and therefore less likely. Removing the utensils from the child's reach further decreases the likelihood of inappropriate play.

Component 9: Removing Toys When the Food Arrives

Once the food arrives, the toys should be removed as quickly and efficiently as possible. It would be wise with younger children for the parents to either take the toys themselves or have the children hand the toys to them. Praising this behavior as well as all other appropriate behaviors is a good management tool.

Component 10: Praising Appropriate Behavior

Parents should praise children when they behave appropriately. If the parents desire a more tangible form of reinforcement for the occurrence of appropriate behaviors, a point or token system can be designed (discussed later).

Some parents may need practice in spotting and praising appropriate behavior, since they have become so used to doing the opposite, that is, spotting and disapproving (sometimes vehemently) of inappropriate behavior. In role-play situations, the clinician can have the parents practice some of the following key phrases, so that the words begin to feel comfortable:

"I like the way you're sitting in your seat!"
"You did a great job keeping your hands and feet to yourself. Everyone appreciates your restraint."
"Thank you for not playing with your spoon and fork."
"Your table manners are excellent."

Table 3.   Unacceptable behaviors for dining out

===

1. Inappropriate verbal behavior, including crying, whining, demanding, interrupting others, humming, and singing
2. Inappropriate motor behavior, including standing on a chair, being out of the chair without permission, hitting or kicking others, and reaching more than halfway across the table
3. Inappropriate use of food or utensils, including picking up nonfinger foods with hands, playing with dinner utensils, and stuffing, dropping, or tossing food into the mouth
4. Noncompliance with a parental request

"I like it when you don't stuff your mouth with food and try to talk at the same time."

☐ An Additional Component of the Advice Package: Stipend Plus Fine

As in the shopping advice package, a family may consider using an additional tangible reinforcer for the display of appropriate behaviors during the premeal restaurant experience. (Refer to Chapter 8 for details on implementing a stipend plus fine program.) Briefly, each child is given a stipend at the beginning of the outing. Contingent on the occurrence of specified undesirable behaviors when dining out, the child loses a certain amount as a fine. Before implementing the stipend plus fine component, the clinician should initially identify unacceptable dining behavior with parent input.

The specification of unacceptable dining behaviors can be taken from the study by Baumann and colleagues (1983). Behaviors can be added or deleted with parental input for each child. Table 3 lists the unacceptable behaviors described in that study.

Implemention of the stipend plus fine component should be considered only after the advice package described earlier has been in effect for multiple restaurant visits. This allows the advice package to produce an increase in appropriate behavior, leaving a smaller level of problem behaviors to be dealt with through the stipend plus fine component. The clinician must stress to the parents that the stipend and fine component should not be used in isolation. Given the nature of restaurants, the best way to deal with inappropriate behavior is to set up conditions under which inappropriate behavior becomes unlikely. This is accomplished by following the 10 components of the advice package.

Table 4.   Stipend and fine program

Date: _____
The following behaviors result in a fine on each occurrence
                    [list those you wish to use by examining Table 3]:
   playing with utensils
   playing with food
   not keeping hands and feet to self

The following stipend amounts and fine amounts for this trip are applicable for each child:

Name	Stipend Amount	Fine Amount
S.T.	$5.00	$1.00
U.T.	$3.00	$0.50
A.T.	$1.00	$0.10

Similar procedures can be used to implement the stipend and fine system for the premeal period as those advocated in Chapter 8. The child can spend his or her savings on the next trip if not more than half the stipend was lost. Also, parents might consider allowing the child to buy a special dessert on the next trip with the money earned or might require a portion of the cost of the dessert to be paid by the child.

The form in Table 4 illustrates the stipend plus fine program for three children. The form specifies the behaviors, the amount of the initial stipend, and the amount of the fines for each child (assuming different ages for each child). For each occurrence of a behavior specified in Table 4, the relevant amount of the fine is subtracted from the stipend.

Table 5 is a hypothetical example of a restaurant outing and the fines administered for each child. Each time a fine is levied, the next number is circled. To arrive at the fine amount, the last number circled is multiplied by the fine amount. In this example, S.T. was fined three times and lost $3.00, ending with $2.00. U.T. was fined four times during the shopping trip, losing $2.00, but A.T. was not fined at all (kept entire $1.00 stipend).

☐ Possible Questions Concerning the Advice Package

Once the advice package has been explained to the parents, questions and issues may arise. A few possible questions and suggestions for responding to them follow.

Table 5.   Stipend card

| Child: S.T. | | Child: U.T. | | Child: A.T. | |
Stipend: $5.00		Stipend: $3.00		Stipend: $1.00	
①		①		1	
②		②		2	
③		③		3	
4		④		4	
5		5		5	
		6		6	
				7	
				8	
				9	
				10	
Fine amount	$3.00	Balance	$1.00	Balance	$1.00

Question 1: What types of restaurants should we use this advice package in?

Because the premeal time is the critical period in which most problems occur, restaurants that take a long time to prepare food are not the best settings to kick off the program. Those that serve already prepared food have a shorter premeal time and thereby allow the parents to make success more possible. Restaurants in which the premeal time is 5 to 10 minutes are preferable in the beginning. As the family gets used to interacting in a manner designated by the advice package, restaurants that take longer to serve food can be visited, with the maintenance of good results more likely.

Question 2: Will it be necessary for us always to interact and engage the children during premeal time to reduce problem behavior?

This advice package is labor-intensive. Especially in the beginning, parents will find that it takes time and energy to engage the children in appropriate behavior during the premeal time. As the children get practiced at this routine, however, they will probably require less time from the parents. Parental effort to engage the children will become less and less over time. Also, many parents find that engaging the children during this time is pleasant and enjoyable in and of itself. It may be one of the few instances (especially in families with hectic schedules) that the family spends quality time together.

Question 3: Once we use the advice package and it works, should we always take our children out to dine with us?

Obviously, this is up to personal choice. However, there are times when parents need to be out by themselves for the sake of their relationship. Perhaps answering this question by saying it is a matter of choice, but that it is not a sin to dine out without children, is the wisest response.

☐ Summary

The advice package offered in this chapter consists of a number of components that make unacceptable child behavior less probable by providing a host of activities during the premeal time and by removing the opportunity to engage in unacceptable behaviors. It received empirical verification as a package that could work with families and is feasible to use in restaurants.

The following two scenarios illustrate what a family restaurant outing might look like before and after the family implemented the advice package.

Before

Mr. and Mrs. M. take their three children—aged 7, 4, and 3—to a family-style restaurant. The car trip there seems to indicate that they will have to keep their wits about them during the restaurant experience. Before they go into the restaurant, Mrs. M. turns to the children and says, "Behave or else!"

They enter the restaurant and are seated at a table in the middle of the rest of the customers. The children are seated next to each other, and the parents are opposite them. Shortly thereafter, even before the waitress comes, problems occur.

The family sitting next to them has children also, and the M.'s two younger children begin to play hide-and-seek with the other children. The 7-year-old taps his knife against the fork and is aroused by the sound. The two younger ones see this, lose interest in ducking under the table and do the same. Mrs. M. threatens to take away their utensils if they continue but does not. The 3-year-old ends up banging his fork against his finger and then cries profusely. Mrs. M. takes him in her lap and will eventually try to eat her meal while he is still there. The other two children continually leave the table and Mr. M. has to go and get them. He tells them that they are ruining the outing and promises never to take them out to eat again. A few moments later, these two are back to playing with their utensils. Forty-five minutes after they have entered the restaurant, the food comes and the M. family "survives" another outing!

After

Mr. and Mrs. M. plan to go to a family restaurant this evening with their three children. Mr. M. asks each child what they would like for a snack before the meal, offering crackers, cereal, or a piece of fruit. He puts each child's choice in a small brown bag with the child's name on it. Mrs. M. helps each child select one or two toys to play with while waiting for their food.

Mr. and Mrs. M. select a restaurant where the wait will be no longer than 20 minutes after ordering. Before they get to the restaurant, they go over the plan (i.e., the children will get a snack when they sit down then play with toys until the food arrives) and what are appropriate behaviors (e.g., responding to parents' requests, staying seated unless asking to go to bathroom, leaving utensils alone until it is time to eat).

When the family arrives at the restaurant, they request a booth away from the crowd. The two younger children are seated next to the wall, with Mrs. M. between them. Mr. M. sits with the older child on the opposite side and immediately moves all the utensils to his area, out of reach of the children. Mr. M. distributes the snack bags. When the children finish, Mrs. M. asks each which toy he or she wants to play with. Mr. M. engages his 7-year-old son in a spelling game. When the food comes, the toys are quickly gathered up, the utensils are put where they belong, and the family begins to eat. Peace has come to the Martinez family outing. They might actually look forward to their next family trip to a restaurant!

Afterword

This book provided practical information on the use of child behavioral consultation in clinical practice. Specific plans were offered in the last two parts of the book about tackling specific problem areas and using specific behavioral strategies. Clinicians may now feel ready to use this information for the betterment of the families they serve.

It is important to develop a mindset when using behavioral techniques, one that is characteristic of people who are very good at engineering behavior change. Here are the top 10 attitudes of successful behavioral consultants.

Top 10 Attitudes of
Successful Behavioral Consultants or Clinicians

10. They start with small steps.
 9. They build on small successes.
 8. They don't accept easy excuses for not trying.
 7. If they don't succeed at first, they don't quit.
 6. They have confidence in their skills.
 5. They commit to a behavioral approach to solving child problems.
 4. They seek out additional training in behavioral consultation.
 3. They take pride in their ability to engineer child behavior change.
 2. They consult others who may have more experience when they get stuck.
 1. They believe they can make a difference.

References

Bailey, J. S., Wolf, M. M., & Phillips, E. L. (1970). Home-based reinforcement and the modification of pre-delinquents' classroom behavior. *Journal of Applied Behavior Analysis, 3,* 223–233.

Baumann, K. E., Reiss, M. L., Rogers, R. W., & Bailey, J. S. (1983). Dining out with children: Effectiveness of a parent advice package on pre-meal inappropriate behavior. *Journal of Applied Behavior Analysis, 16,* 55–68.

Cipani, E. (1994). Treating children's severe behavior disorders: A behavioral diagnostic system. *Journal of Behavior Therapy and Experimental Psychiatry, 25,* 293–300.

Clark, H. B., Greene, B. F., MacRae, J. W., McNees, M. P., Davis, J. L., & Risley, T. R. (1977). A parent advice package for family shopping trips: Development and evaluation. *Journal of Applied Behavior Analysis, 10,* 605–624.

Green, R. B., Harbison, W. L., & Greene, B. F. (1984). Turning the table on advice programs for parents: Using placemats to enhance family interaction at restaurants. *Journal of Applied Behavior Analysis, 17,* 497–508.

Iwata, B. A., & Bailey, J. S. (1974). Reward versus cost token systems: An analysis of the effects on students and teacher. *Journal of Applied Behavior Analysis, 7,* 567–576.

Mace, F. C., Hock, H. L., Lalli, J. S., West, B. J., Belfiore, P., Pinter, E., & Brown, D. K. (1988). Behavioral momentum in the treatment of noncompliance. *Journal of Applied Behavior Analysis, 21,* 123–141.

Porterfield, J. K., Herbert-Jackson, E., & Risley, T. R. (1976). Contingent observation: An effective and acceptable procedure for reducing disruptive behavior of young children in a group setting. *Journal of Applied Behavior Analysis, 9,* 55–64.

Related Books

Baker, B. L., Brightman, A. J., Heifetz, L. J., & Murphy, D. M. (1976). *Behavior problems.* Champaign, IL: Research Press.

Becker, W. C. (1971). *Parents are teachers: A child management program.* Champaign, IL: Research Press.

Blechman, E. A. (1985). *Solving child behavior problems at home and school.* Champaign, IL: Research Press.

Burke, R. V., & Herron, R. W. (1992). *Common sense parenting.* Boys Town, NE: Father Flanagan's Boys's Home.

Cipani, E. (Ed.). (1989). *Treating severe behavior disorders: Behavior analysis approaches.* Washington, DC: American Association on Mental Retardation.

Cipani, E. (1993). *Disruptive behavior: Three techniques to use in your classroom.* Reston, VA: Council for Exceptional Children.

Cipani, E. (1993). *Non-compliance: Four strategies that work.* Reston, VA: Council for Exceptional Children.

Cipani, E. (1998). *Classroom Management for all teachers: Eleven effective plans.* Columbus, OH: Prentice-Hall.

Coughlin, E., & Shanahan, D. (1988). *Boys Town family home program.* Boys Town, NE: Father Flanagan's Boys' home.

Forehand, R., & McMahon, R. J. (1981). *Helping the noncompliant child: A clinician's guide to parent training.* New York: Guilford Press.

Goldstein, A. P., Keller, H., & Erne, D. (1985). *Changing the abusive parent.* Champaign, IL: Research Press.

Hall, R. V., & Hall, M. C. (Series Ed.). *How to manage behavior series* (Vol. 1–12). Austin, TX: Pro-Ed.

Kaplan, J. S., & Kamperman, M. G. (1996). *Kid Mod.* Austin, TX: Pro-Ed.

Kazdin, A. E. (1984). *Behavior modification in applied settings* (3rd ed.). Homewood, IL: Dorsey.

Lavelle, L. (1988). *Practical charts for managing behavior.* Austin, TX: Pro-Ed.

Parker, H. C. (1991). *Goal card program.* Columbia: MO: Hawthorne Educational Services, Inc.

Patterson, G. R. (1976). *Living with children: New methods for parents and teachers.* Champaign, IL: Research Press.

Shapiro, E. S., & Cole, C. L. (1994). *Behavior change in the classroom: Self-management interventions.* Columbia, MO: Hawthorne Educational Services, Inc.

Sloane, H. N. (1988). *The good kid book: How to solve the 16 most common behavior problems.* Champaign, IL: Research Press.

Walker, H. M., & Walker, J. E. (1991). *Coping with non-compliance in the classroom: A positive approach for teachers.* Austin, TX: Pro-Ed.

Workman, E. A., & Katz, A. M. (1995). *Teaching behavioral self-control to students.* (2nd ed.). Austin, TX: Pro-Ed.

B
APPENDIX

Behavioral Parent Training References

Baker, B. L., & Brightman, R. P. (1984). Training parents of retarded children: Program-specific outcomes. *Journal of Behavior Therapy and Experimental Psychiatry, 15,* 255–260.

Ball, T. S., Coyne, A., Jarvis, R. M., & Pease, S. S. F. (1984). Parents of retarded children as teaching assistants for other parents. *Education and Training of the Mentally Retarded, 19,* 64–69.

Bank, L., Marlowe, J. H., Reid, J. B., Patterson, G. R., & Weinrott, M. R. (1991). A comparative evaluation of parent-training interventions for families of chronic delinquents. *Journal of Abnormal Child Psychology, 19*(1), 15–33.

Barone, V. J., Greene, B. F., & Lutzker, J. R. (1986). Home safety with families being treated for child abuse and neglect. *Behavior Modification, 10,* 93–114.

Bernal, M. E., Klinnert, M. D., & Schultz, L. A. (1980). Outcome evaluation of behavioral parent training and client-centered parent counseling for children with conduct problems. *Journal of Applied Behavior Analysis, 13,* 677–691.

Bollard, J., Nettlebeck, T., & Roxbee, L. (1982). Dry-bed training for childhood bedwetting: A comparison of group with individually administered parent instruction. *Behavior Research and Therapy, 20,* 209–217.

Brody, G. H., & Forehand, R. (1985). The efficacy of parent training with maritally distressed and nondistressed mothers: A multimethod assessment. *Behaviour Research and Therapy, 23,* 291–296.

Brownell, K. D., Kelman, J. H., & Stunkard, A. J. (1983). Treatment of obese children with and without their mothers: Changes in weight and blood pressure. *Pediatrics, 71,* 515–523.

Budd, K. S., Madison, L. S., Iztkowitz, J. S., George, C. H., & Price, H. A. (1986). Parents and therapist as allies in behavioral treatment of children's stuttering. *Behavior Therapy, 17,* 538–553.

Bunyan, A. (1987). "Help, I can't cope with my child": A behavioral approach to the treatment of a conduct disordered child within the natural homesetting. *British Journal of Social Work, 17,* 237–256.

165

Calvert, S. C., & McMahon, R. J. (1987). The treatment acceptability of a behavioral parent training program and its components. *Behavior Therapy, 18,* 165–179.

Campbell, R. V., O'Brien, S., Bickett, A. D., & Lutzker, J. R. (1983). In-home parent training, treatment of migraine headaches, and marital counseling as an ecobehavioral approach to prevent child abuse. *Journal of Behavior Therapy and Experimental Psychiatry, 14,* 147–154.

Chadez, L. H., & Nurius, P. S. (1987). Stopping bedtime crying: Treating the child and the parents. *Journal of Clinical Child Psychology, 16,* 212–217.

Christensen, A., Johnson, S. M., Phillips, S., & Glasgow, R. E. (1980). Cost effectiveness in behavioral family therapy. *Behavior Therapy, 11,* 208–226.

Christophersen, E. R., Barnard, J. D., Ford, D., & Wolf, M. M. (1976). The family training program: Improving parent-child interactions. In E. J. Mash, L. C. Handy, & C. A. Hamerlvnck (Eds.), *Behavior modification approaches to parenting.* New York: Brunner/Mazel.

Cipani, E. (1984). A behavioral model for the delivery of technical assistance in the home. *Child Care Quarterly, 13,* 177–192.

Cipani, E. (1985). The three phases of behavioral consultation: Objectives, intervention, and quality assurance. *Teacher Education and Special Education, 8,* 144–152.

Clark, D. B., & Baker, B. L. (1983). Predicting outcomes in parent training. *Journal of Consulting and Clinical Psychology, 51,* 309–311.

Crimmins, D. B., Bradlyn, A. S., St. Lawrence, J. S., & Kelly, J. A. (1984). A training technique for improving the parent-child interaction skills of an abusive-neglectful mother. *Child Abuse and Neglect, 8,* 533–539.

Dadds, M. R., Sanders, M. R., & James, J. E. (1987). The generalization of treatment effects in parent training with multidistressed parents. *Behavioural Psychotherapy, 15,* 289–313.

Dadds, M. R., Schwartz, S., & Sanders, M. R. (1987). Marital discord and treatment outcome in behavioral treatment of child conduct disorders. *Journal of Consulting and Clinical Psychology, 55,* 396–403.

Daly, R. M., Holland, C. J., Forrest, P. A., & Felbaum, G. A. (1985). Temporal generalization of treatment effects over a three-year period for a parent training program: Directive parental counseling (DPC). *Canadian Journal of Behavioural Sciences, 17,* 379–388.

Dangle, R. F., & Polster, R. A. (1984). Winning!: A systematic, empirical approach to parent training. In R. A. Polster & R. F. Dangle (Eds.), *Parent training: Foundations of research and practice* (pp. 162–201). New York: The Guilford Press.

Dishion, T. J., & Patterson, G. R. (1992). Age effects in parent training outcome. *Behavior Therapy, 23,* 719–729.

Dubey, D. R., O'Leary, S. G., & Kaufman, K. F. (1983). Training parents of hyperactive children in child management: A comparative outcome study. *Journal of Abnormal Child Psychology, 11,* 229–246.

Dumas, J. E. (1984). Child, adult-interactional, and socioeconomic setting events as predictors of parent-training outcome. *Education and Treatment of Children, 7,* 351–363.

Dumas, J. E. (1984). Interactional correlates of treatment outcome in behavioral parent training. *Journal of Consulting and Clinical Psychology, 52,* 946–954.

Dumas, J. E., & Albin, J. B. (1986). Parent training outcome: Does active parental involvement matter? *Behaviour Research and Therapy, 24,* 227–230.

Dumas, J. E., & Lechowicz, J. G. (1989). When do noncompliant children comply? Implications for family behavior therapy. *Child and Family Behavior Therapy, 11,* 21–38.

Dumas, J. E., & Wahler, R. G. (1983). Predictors of treatment outcome in parent training: Mother insularity and socioeconomic disadvantage. *Behavioral Assessment, 5,* 301–313.

Dumas, J. E.,. & Wahler, R. G. (1985). Indiscriminate mothering as a contextual factor in aggressive-oppositional child behavior: "Damned if you do and damned if you don't!" *Journal of Abnormal Child Psychology, 13,* 1–17.

Egan, K. J. (1983). Stress management and child management with abusive parents. *Journal of Clinical Child Psychology, 12,* 292–299.

Eyberg, S. M., & Boggs, S. R. (1989). Parent training for oppositional defiant preschoolers. In C. E. Schaefer & J. M. Briesmeister (Eds.), *Handbook of parent training.* New York: John Wiley and Sons.

Eyberg, S. M., & Robinson, E. A. (1982). Parent-child interaction training: Effects on family functioning. *Journal of Clinical Child Psychology, 11,* 130–137.

Feldman, J. M., & Kazdin, A. E. (1995). Parent management training for oppositional and conduct problem children. *The Clinical Psychologist, 48(4),* 3–4.

Feldman, W. S., Manella, K. J., Apodaca, L., & Varni, J. W. (1982). Behavioral group parent training in spina bifida. *Journal of Clinical Child Psychology, 11,* 144–150.

Feldman, W. S., Manella, K. J., & Varni, J. W. (1983). A behavioural programme for single mothers of physically handicapped children. *Child: Care, Health, and Development 9,* 157–168.

Firestone, P., Crowe, D., Goodman, J. T., & McGrath, P. (1986). Vicissitudes of follow-up studies: Differential effects of parent training and stimulant medication with hyperactives. *American Journal of Orthopsychiatry, 56,* 184–194.

Firestone, P., & Witt, J. E. (1982). Characteristics of families completing and prematurely discontinuing a behavioral parent-training program. *Journal of Pediatric Psychology, 7,* 209–222.

Forehand, R. (1986). Parental positive reinforcement with defiant children: Does it make a difference? *Child and Family Behavior Therapy, 8,* 19–25.

Forehand, R., Furey, W. M., & McMahon, R. J. (1984). The role of maternal distress in a parent training program to modify child noncompliance. *Behavioural Psychotherapy, 12,* 93–108.

Forehand, R., & Kotchick, B. A. (1996). Cultural diversity: A wake-up call for parent training. *Behavior Therapy, 27,* 187–206.

Forehand, R., Rogers, T., McMahon, R. J., Wells, K. C., & Griest, D. L. (1981). Teaching parents to modify child behavior problems: An examination of some follow-up data. *Journal of Pediatric Psychology, 6,* 313–322.

Forehand, R., Steffe, M. A., Furey, W. M., & Walley, P. B. (1983). Mothers' evaluation of a parent training program completed three and one-half years earlier. *Journal of Behavior Therapy and Experimental Psychiatry, 14,* 339–342.

Forrest, P., Holland, C., Daly, R., & Fellbaum, G. A. (1984). When parents become therapists: Their attitudes toward parenting three years later. *Canadian Journal of Community Mental Health, 3,* 49–54.

Furey, W. M., & Basili, L. A. (1988). Predicting consumer satisfaction in parent training for noncompliant children. *Behavior Therapy, 19,* 555–564.

Gaudin, J. M., & Kurtz, D. P. (1985). Parenting skills training for child abusers. *Journal of Group Psychotherapy, Psychodrama, and Sociotherapy, 38,* 35–54.

Giebenhain, J. E., & O'Dell, S. L. (1984). Evaluation of a parent-training manual for reducing children's fears of the dark. *Journal of Applied Behavior Analysis, 17,* 121–125.

Graziano, A. M., & Diament, D. M. (1992). Behavioral parent training: An examination of the paradigm. *Behavior Modification, 16,* 3–38.

Graziano, A. M., & Diament, D. M. (1992). Parent behavioral training: An examination of the paradigm. *Behavior Modification, 16(1),* 3–38.

Graziano, A. M., & Mooney, K. C. (1982). Behavioral treatment of children's "nightfear": A 3-year follow-up. *Journal of Consulting and Clinical Psychology, 50,* 598–599.

Griest, D. L., & Forehand, R. (1982). How can I get any parent training done with all these other problems going on? The role of family variables in child behavior therapy. *Child and Family Behavior Therapy, 4,* 73–80.

Griest, D. L., Forehand, R., Rogers, T., Breiner, J., Furey, W., & Williams, C. A. (1982). Effects of parent enhancement therapy on the treatment outcome and generalization of a parent training program. *Behaviour Research and Therapy, 20,* 429–436.

Griest, D. L., Forehand, R., & Wells, K. C. (1983). Follow-up assessment of parent training: An analysis of who will participate. *Child Study Journal, 11,* 221–229.

Griest, D. L., & Wells, K. C. (1983). Behavioral family therapy with conduct disorders in children. *Behavior Therapy, 14,* 37–53.

Hamilton, S. B., & MacQuiddy, S. L. (1984). Self-administered behavioral parent training: Enhancement of treatment efficacy using a time-out signal seat. *Journal of Clinical Child Psychology, 13,* 61–69.

Harris, S. L. (1986). Brief report: A 4-to-7 year questionnaire follow-up of participants in a training program for parents of autistic children. *Journal of Autism and Developmental Disorders, 16,* 377–383.

Harris, S. L. (1986). Parents as teachers: A four to seven year follow-up of parents of children with autism. *Child and Family Behavior Therapy, 8,* 39–47.

Henry, G. K. (1987). Symbolic modeling and parent behavior training: Effects on noncompliance of hyperactive children. *Journal of Behavior Therapy and Experimental Psychiatry, 18,* 105–113.

Holden, G. W., Lavigne, V. V., & Cameron, A. M. (1990). Probing the continuum of effectiveness in parent training: Characteristics of parents and preschoolers. *Journal of Clinical Child Psychology, 19,* 1–8.

Holmes, N., Hemsley, R., Rickett, J., & Likierman, H. (1982). Parents as co-therapists: Their perceptions of a home-based behavioral treatment for autistic children. *Journal of Autism and Developmental Disorders, 12,* 331–342.

Horn, W. F., Ialongo, N., Popovich, S., & Peradotto, D. (1987). Behavioral parent training and cognitive-behavioral self-control therapy with ADD-H children: Comparative and combined effects. *Journal of Clinical Psychology, 16,* 57–68.

Hornby, G., & Singh, N. N. (1983). Group training for parents of mentally retarded children: A review and methodological analysis of behavioral studies. *Child: Care, Health and Development, 9,* 199–213.

Hornby, G., & Singh, N. N. (1984). Behavioural group training with parents of mentally retarded children. *Journal of Mental Deficiency Research, 28,* 43–52.

Horton, L. (1982). Comparison of instructional components in behavioral parent training. *Behavioral Counseling Quarterly, 2,* 131–147.

Horton, L. (1984). The father's role in behavioral parent training: A review. *Journal of Clinical Child Psychology, 13,* 274–279.

Hudson, A. M. (1982). Training parents of developmentally handicapped children: A component analysis. *Behavior Therapy, 13,* 325–333.

Hughes, R. C., & Wilson, P. H. (1988). Behavioral parent training: Contingency management versus communication skills training with or without participation of the child. *Child and Family Behavior Therapy, 10,* 11–23.

Humphreys, L., Forehand, R., McMahon, R., & Roberts, M. (1978). Parent behavioral training to modify child noncompliance: Effects on untreated siblings. *Journal of Behavior Therapy and Experimental Psychiatry, 9,* 235–238.

Issacs, C. D. (1982). Treatment of child abuse: A review of the behavioral interventions. *Journal of Applied Behavior Analysis, 15,* 273–294.

Israel, A. C., Stolmaker, L., & Andrian, C. A. G. (1985). The effects of training parents in general child management skills on a behavioral weight loss program for children. *Behavior Therapy, 16,* 169–180.

Kashima, K. J., Baker, B., & Landen, S. J. (1988). Media-based versus professionally-led training for parents of mentally retarded children. *American Journal of Mental Retardation, 93,* 209–217.

Kazdin, A. E., Esveldt-Dawson, K., French, N. H., & Unis, A. S. (1987). Effects of parent management training and problem-solving skills training combined in the treatment of antisocial child behavior. *Journal of the American Academy of Child and Adolescent Psychiatry, 36,* 416–424.

Knapp, P. A., & Deluty, R. H. (1989). Relative effectiveness of two behavioral parent training programs. *Journal of Clinical Child Psychology, 18,* 314–322.

Kolko, D. J. (1983). Multicomponent parental treatment of firesetting in a six year old boy. *Journal of Behavior Therapy and Experimental Psychiatry, 14,* 349–353.

Lavigueur, H., Peterson, R. F., Sheese, J. G., & Peterson, L. W. (1973). Behavioral treatment in the home: Effects on an untreated sibling and long-term follow-up. *Behavior Therapy, 4,* 431–441.

Lieh-Mak, F., Lee, P. W. H., & Luk, S. L. (1984). Problems encountered in teaching Chinese parents to be behavior therapists. *Psychologia, 27,* 56–64.

Long, P., Forehand, R., Wierson, M., & Morgan, A. (1994). Does parent training with young noncompliant children have long-term effects? *Behaviour Research and Therapy, 32,* 101–107.

Lowry, M. A., & Whitman, T. L. (1989). Generalization of parenting skills: An early intervention program.

Lutzker, J. R., McGimsey, J. F., McRae, S., & Campbell, R. V. (1983). Behavior parent training: There's so much more to do. *The Behavior Therapist, 6,* 110–113.

McAuley, R. (1982). Training parents to modify conduct problems in their children. *Journal of Child Psychology and Psychiatry, 23,* 335–342.

McDonald, M. R., & Budd, K. S. (1983). "Booster shots" following didactic parent training: Effects of follow-up using graphic feedback and instructions. *Behavior Modification, 7,* 211–223.

McLoughlin, C. S. (1982). Procedures and problems in behavioral training for parents. *Perceptual and Motor Skills, 55,* 827–838.

McMahon, R. J., & Forehand, R. L. (1983). Consumer satisfaction in behavioral treatment of children: Types, issues, and recommendations. *Behavior Therapy, 14,* 209–225.

McMahon, R. J., Forehand, R., Griest, D. L., & Wells, K. C. (1981). Who drops out of therapy during parent behavioral training. *Behavior Counseling Quarterly, 1,* 79–85.

McMahon, R. J., Tiedemann, G. L., & Forehand, R., & Griest, D. L. (1984). Parental satisfaction with parent training to modify child noncompliance. *Behavior Therapy, 15,* 295–303.

McMenamy, C., & Katz, R. C. (1989). Brief parent-assisted treatment for children's nighttime fears. *Journal of Developmental and Behavior Pediatrics, 10,* 145–148.

Moreland, J. R., Schwebel, A. I., Beck, S., & Wells, R. (1982). Parents as therapists: A review of the behavior therapy parent training literature—1975 to 1981. *Behavior Modification, 6,* 250–276.

Muir, K. A., & Milan, M. A. (1982). Parent reinforcement for child achievement: The use of a lottery to maximize parent training effects. *Journal of Applied Behavior Analysis, 15,* 455–460.

O'Dell, S. (1974). Training parents in behavior modification: A review. *Psychological Bulletin, 81,* 418–433.

O'Dell, S. L., O'Quin, J. A., Alford, B. A., O'Briant, A. L., Bradlyn, A. S., & Giegehain, J. E. (1982). Predicting the acquisition of parenting skills via four training models. *Behavior Therapy, 13,* 194–208.

Patterson, G. R., Chamberlain, P., & Reid, J. B. (1982). A comparative evaluation of a parent-training program. *Behavior Therapy, 13,* 638–650.

Pevsner, R. (1982). Group parent training versus individual family therapy: An outcome study. *Behavior Therapy and Experimental Psychiatry, 13,* 119–122.

Pollard, S., Ward, E. M., & Barkley, R. A. (1983). The effects of parent training and Ritalin on the parent-child interactions of hyperactive boys. *Child and Family Therapy, 5,* 51–69.

Prieto-Bayard, M., & Baker, B. L. (1986). Parent training for Spanish-speaking families with a retarded child. *Journal of Community Psychology, 14,* 134–143.

Reisinger, J. J. (1982). Unprogrammed learning of differential attention of fathers of oppositional children. *Journal of Behavior Therapy and Experimental Psychiatry, 13,* 203–208.

Rickert, V. I., Sottolano, D. C. , Parrish, J. M., Riley, A. W., Hunt, F. M., & Pelco, L. E. (1988). Training parents to become better behavior managers: The need for a competency-based approach. *Behavior Modification, 12,* 475–496.

Rios, J. D., & Gutierrez, J. M. (1986). Parent training with non-traditional families: An unresolved issue. *Child and Family Behavior Therapy, 7,* 33–45.

Rogers-Weise, M. R. (1992). A critical review of parent training research. *Psychology in the Schools, 29,* 229–236.

Rosenberg, M. S., & Repucci, N. D. (1985). Primary prevention of child abuse. *Journal of Consulting and Clinical Psychology, 53,* 576–585.

Ruma, P. R., Burke, R. V., & Thompson, R. W. (1996). Group parent training: Is it effective for children of all ages? *Behavior Therapy, 27,* 159–169.

Sanders, M. R. (1982). The effects of instructions, feedback and cueing procedures in behavioural parent training. *Australian Journal of Psychology, 34,* 53–69.

Sanders, M. R. (1992). New directions in behavioral family intervention with children: From clinical management to prevention. *New Zealand Journal of Psychology, 21,* 25–36.

Sanders, M. R., & Christensen, A. P. (1985). A comparison of the effects of child management and planned activities training in five parenting environments. *Journal of Abnormal Child Psychology, 13,* 101–117.

Sanders, M. R.,. & Dadds, M. R. (1982). The effects of planned activities and child management procedures in parent training: An analysis of setting generality. *Behavior Therapy, 13,* 452–461.

Sanders, M. R., & James, J. E. (1983). The modification of parent behavior: A review of generalization and maintenance. *Behavior Modification, 7,* 3–27.

Sanders, M. R., & Plant, K. (1989). Programming for generalization to high and low risk parenting situations in families with oppositional, developmentally delayed preschool children. *Behavior Modification, 13,* 283–305.

Sandler, A., Coren, A., & Thurman, S. K. (1983). A training program for parents of handicapped preschool children: Effects upon mother, father, and child. *Exceptional Children, 49,* 355–358.

Scott, M. J., & Stradling, S. G. (1987). Evaluation of a group programme for parents of problem children. *Behavioural Psychotherapy, 15,* 224–239.

Serketich, W. J., Dumas, J. E. (1996). The effectiveness of behavioral parent training to modify antisocial behavior in children: A meta-analysis. *Behavior Therapy, 27,* 171–186.

Sloane, H. N., Endo, G. T., Hawkes, T. W., & Jensen, W. R. (1990). Decreasing children's fighting through self-instructional parent training materials. *School Psychology International, 11,* 17–29.

Thompson, R. W., Grow, C. R., Ruma, P. R., Daly, D. L., & Burke, R. V. (1993). Evaluation of a practical parenting program with middle-and-low income families. *Family Relations, 42,* 21–25.

Twardosz, S., & Nordquist, V. M. (1987). Parent training. In M. Hersen & V. B. Van Hasselt (Eds.), *Behavior therapy with children and adolescents: A clinical approach* (pp. 75–105). New York: Wiley.

Van Hasselt, V. B., Sisson, L. A., & Aach, S. R. (1987). Parent training to increase compliance in a young multihandicapped child. *Journal of Behavior Therapy and Experimental Psychiatry, 18,* 275–283.

Wahler, R. G. (1980). The insular mother: Her problems in parent-child treatment. *Journal of Behavior Therapy and Experimental Psychiatry, 18,* 207–219.

Walle, D. L., Hobbs, S. A., & Caldwell, H. S. (1984). Sequencing of parent training procedures: Effects on child noncompliance and treatment acceptability. *Behavior Modification, 8,* 540–552.

Webster-Stratton, C. (1982). The long-term effects of a videotape modeling parent-training program: Comparison of immediate and 1-year follow-up results. *Behavior Therapy, 13,* 702–714.

Webster-Stratton, C. (1982). Teaching mothers through viedotape modeling to change their children's behavior. *Journal of Pediatric Psychiatry, 7,* 279–294.

Webster-Stratton, C. (1984). Randomized trial of two parent-training programs with conduct-disordered children. *Journal of Consulting and Clinical Psychology, 52,* 666–678.

Webster-Stratton, C. (1985). The effects of father involvement in parent training for conduct problem children. *Journal of Child Psychiatry and Psychology, 26,* 801–810.

Webster-Stratton, C. (1985). Predictors of treatment outcome in parent training for conduct disordered children. *Behavior Therapy, 16,* 223–243.

Webster-Stratton, C. (1992). Individually administered videotape parent-training: "Who benefits?" *Cognitive Therapy and Research, 16,* 31–35.

Webster-Stratton, C., & Hammond, M. (1990). Predictors of treatment outcome for parent training for families with conduct problem children. *Behavior Therapy, 21,* 319–337.

Webster-Stratton, C., Hollinsworth, T., & Kolpacoff, M. (1989). The long-term effectiveness and clinical significance of three cost-effective training programs for families with conduct-problem children. *Journal of Consulting and Clinical Psychology, 57,* 550–553.

Webster-Stratton, C., Kolpacoff, M., & Hollinsworth, T. (1988). The long-term effectiveness and clinical significance of three cost-effective training programs for families with conduct-problem children. *Journal of Consulting and Clinical Psychology, 57,* 550–553.

Webster-Stratton, C., Kolpacoff, M., & Hollinsworth, T. (1988). Self-administered video tape therapy for families with conduct-problem children: Comparison with two cost-effective treatments and a control group. *Journal of Consulting and Clinical Psychology, 56,* 558–566.

Wiese, M. R., & Kramer, J. J. (1988). Parent training research: An analysis of the empirical literature, 1975–1985. *Psychology in the Schools, 25,* 325–330.

Wolfe, D. A., Edwards, B., Manion, I., & Koverola, C. (1988). Early intervention for parents at risk of child abuse and neglect: A preliminary investigation. *Journal of Consulting and Clinical Psychology, 56,* 40–47.

Wolfe, D. A., St. Lawrence, J., Graves, K., Brehony, K., Bradlyn, D., & Kelly, J. A. (1982). Intensive behavior parent training for a child abusive mother. *Behavior Therapy, 13,* 438–451.

Zangwill, W. N. (1983). An evaluation of a parent training program. *Child and Family Behavior Therapy, 5,* 1–16.

C

APPENDIX

Clinical Forms*

This appendix contains clinical forms for the following chapters:

Chapter 2: The Five Phases of a Behavioral Consultation Model
Chapter 4: Behavioral Momentum: An Effective Technique for Gaining Compliance in Young Children.
Chapter 5: The Noncompliance Barometer and Compliance With Older Children
Chapter 6: parent Solution for School-Related Problems: The Daily Report Card.
Chapter 7: The Effective Use of Time-Out for Disruptive Behavior
Chapter 8: Shopping Trips Can Be Pleasant
Chapter 9: An Advice Package for Dining Out at Family Restaurants

These forms include intake information forms, data collection forms, and parent handouts on the plan designated in the chapter.

*Erika Blinn is acknowledged for her review and comments on an earlier draft of this appendix.

☐ **Chapter 2**

==

FORM 1.   Parent report of child problem behaviors: Intake information

==

Child: _____

Date: _____

Parent(s) interviewed: _____

For each behavior under the following three sections, ask the parent to (1) estimate the level of the behavior (by circling N, S, or O for each behavior (using key below) and (2) indicate the perceived severity by circling H or L in the last column (using the key below).

Estimated level of problem

Key: N = never occurs   H = High
       S = seldom occurs   L = Low
       O = often occurs

Estimated Level			Behaviors	Perceived Severity	
Compliance problems					
N	S	O	Completes activities	H	L
N	S	O	Puts away toys—toys placed back in toy chest, or shelves, or in toy room	H	L
N	S	O	Cleans up room—dirty clothes off the floor or in a hamper; clean shirts and pants hung up or in dresser drawer; garbage in garbage can	H	L
N	S	O	Responds to first request issued	H	L
N	S	O	Independently performs assigned chores	H	L
N	S	O	Complies with "do" commands	H	L
N	S	O	Complies with "don't" commands	H	L

FORM 1. *Continued*

Other problem behavior

N	S	O	Interrupts others in conversations—verbally interjects during conversation between two or more people; does not wait for one person to end their conversation; does not say "excuse me"	H	L
N	S	O	Uses verbal profanity	H	L
N	S	O	Is aggressive against parents	H	L
N	S	O	Is aggressive against peers	H	L
N	S	O	Is aggressive against siblings	H	L
N	S	O	Is aggressive against other adults	H	L
N	S	O	Grabs things from others (without asking)	H	L
N	S	O	Has tantrums—screams, hollers, kicks legs while on floor, whines, kicks or hits property	H	L
N	S	O	runs in house	H	L
N	S	O	Makes excessive noise; vocalization	H	L
N	S	O	Bosses others	H	L
N	S	O	Destroys own property	H	L
N	S	O	Destroys other property	H	L

Other problems not mentioned

N	S	O	_____	H	L
N	S	O	_____	H	L

See Table 2 in Chapter 2 for example.

FORM 2.   Data sheet for monitoring activity completed

Child: _____
Parent(S) recording date: _____
Activity to be completed: _____
Time limit: _____or
*time by which activity is to be completed (e.g., 4:00 P.M.)*_____

Fill out the above information, including the target activity. Have the parent specify the date in the first column, the parent circles a *yes* if the activity was completed or *no* if not completed each day the activity is to be completed.

Date	Activity Completed?	
_____	Yes	No
_____	Yes	No
_____	Yes	No
_____	Yes	No
_____	Yes	No
_____	Yes	No
_____	Yes	No
_____	Yes	No
_____	Yes	No
_____	Yes	No

See Table 3 in Chapter 2 for example.

FORM 3. Data sheet for spot checks

Child: _____

Activity: _____

Designed time (s): _____

Have the parent specify the date of the spot check and (up to 7 possible checks), to indicate whether the child was engaged in the activity (circle the +) or not (circle the −) for each spot check he or she conducts. Determine the percentage of engagement for each date at the end (i.e., number of +'s over the total, +'s and −'s).

				Spot Checks					% Engagement
Date	1	2	3	4	5	6	7		
_____	+ −	+ −	+ −	+ −	+ −	+ −	+ −		_____
_____	+ −	+ −	+ −	+ −	+ −	+ −	+ −		_____
_____	+ −	+ −	+ −	+ −	+ −	+ −	+ −		_____
_____	+ −	+ −	+ −	+ −	+ −	+ −	+ −		_____
_____	+ −	+ −	+ −	+ −	+ −	+ −	+ −		_____
_____	+ −	+ −	+ −	+ −	+ −	+ −	+ −		_____
_____	+ −	+ −	+ −	+ −	+ −	+ −	+ −		_____
_____	+ −	+ −	+ −	+ −	+ −	+ −	+ −		_____
_____	+ −	+ −	+ −	+ −	+ −	+ −	+ −		_____
_____	+ −	+ −	+ −	+ −	+ −	+ −	+ −		_____

See Table 5 in Chapter 2 for example.

FORM 4.   Data sheet for frequency counts

Child: _____

Parent(s)recording data: _____

Date: _____

Deisgnate the child's behaviors in the first column. Record the occurrence of each behavior as it happens. Each time the behavior occurs, the parent circles the next number in the appropriate row (up to 10 occurrences). Each day requires a new data sheet.

Behaviors   **Frequency**

_____	1	2	3	4	5	6	7	8	9	10
_____	1	2	3	4	5	6	7	8	9	10
_____	1	2	3	4	5	6	7	8	9	10
_____	1	2	3	4	5	6	7	8	9	10
_____	1	2	3	4	5	6	7	8	9	10
_____	1	2	3	4	5	6	7	8	9	10

See Table 7 in Chapter 2 for example.

FORM 5.   Data sheet for occurrence/nonoccurrence method

This form can record up to 20 intervals of data. After each interval, if the behavior occurred at all during the interval, the parent circles O (for occurrence). If it did not occur, he or she circles the NO for that interval. This is done for each interval, moving to the next interval with the passage of time.

Date: _____

Child: _____

Parent(s) recording data: _____

Targeted behavior: _____

Setting: _____

Lenth of session: _____

Interval length: _____

Key:

O = occurrence

NO = Nonoccurrence

Interval	Occurence	Nonoccurrence
1		NO
2	O	NO
3	O	NO
4	O	NO
5	O	NO
6	O	NO
7	O	NO
8	O	NO
9	O	NO
10	O	NO
11	O	NO
12	O	NO
13	O	NO
14	O	NO
15	O	NO
16	O	NO
17	O	NO
18	O	NO
19	O	NO
20	O	NO

See Table 8 in Chapter 2 for example.

FORM 6.   Estimated rate of behavior

Child: _____

Parent(s) reporting estimated rate: _____

Date of interview: _____

For each targeted behavior, ask the parent to estimate the rate of the behavior as falling in one of the five categories delineated.

Targeted behavior #1: _____

Does it occur?

_____ 1–10 times/month

_____ 1–10 times/week

_____ 1–10 times/day

_____ 1–10 times/hour

_____ Greater than 10 times/hour

Targeted behavior #2: _____

Does it occur?

_____ 1–10 times/month

_____ 1–10 times/week

_____ 1–10 times/day

_____ 1–10 times/hour

_____ Greater than 10 times/hour

Targeted behavior #3: _____

Does it occur?

_____ 1–10 times/month

_____ 1–10 times/week

_____ 1–10 times/day

_____ 1–10 times/hour

_____ Greater than 10 times/hour

See estimate of behavior in text.

FORM 7.   Previous strategies tried

Child: _____

Parent(s) reporting estimated rate: _____

Behavior (s): _____

Have the parent identify what strategies s/he have tried; what did the procedure involve, and identify it if it was effective, at least in the short term.

Technique or Discipline Strategy	What Did It Involve?	Was it Effective?
_____	_____	_____
_____	_____	_____
_____	_____	_____

See Table 11 in Chapter 2 for example.

FORM 8.   Behavioral objectives

Child's name: _____

Parrent(s):_____

Date: _____

Therapy timeline (in sessions): _____

Objectives (Child's Behavior)

1.
2.
3.
4.
5.

FORM 9.   Progress evaluation and behavioral objectives

Child's name: _____
Parent(s): _____
Date: _____
Therapy timeline (in sessions): _____

Objectives (child's behavior)	Objective Met?	
1.	Yes	No
2.	Yes	No
3.	Yes	No
4.	Yes	No
5.	Yes	No

☐ **Chapter 4**

FORM 1.   Parental commands and instructions that create child compliance problems: Interview form

---

Child: _____

Parent(s): _____

Interview date: _____

Have the parent indicate the circumstances and the particular commands that are given to the child on an everyday basis and then indicate the estimated proability of compliance to that command across a 1 or 2-week period (using the key below).

Key: N = almost never   (0%–25%)
      S = sometimes compliant   (26%–50%)
      F = fair compliance   (51%–75%)
      U = usually compliant   (76%–100%)

Circumstance	**Particular Command**	**Probability of Compliance**			
1.	_____	N	S	F	U
2.	_____	N	S	F	U
3.	_____	N	S	F	U
4.	_____	N	S	F	U
5.	_____	N	S	F	U

See Table 1 in Chapter 4 for example.

FORM 2.   Noncompliance data sheet

Child: _____
Age: _____
Parent(s): _____
Date: _____

Have the parent record commands or instruction he or she identified as problems on Form 1 (category N, S, or F). Each time that command is given, the parent records the time it was given and whether child compliance occurred (by circling *yes* or *no* in Compliance column). A new form is used each day data are recorded.

Command or Instruction	Time Given	Compliance	
1.	_____	Yes	No
	_____	Yes	No
	_____	Yes	No
	_____	Yes	No
2.	_____	Yes	No
	_____	Yes	No
	_____	Yes	No
	_____	Yes	No
3.	_____	Yes	No
	_____	Yes	No
	_____	Yes	No
	_____	Yes	No
4.	_____	Yes	No
	_____	Yes	No
	_____	Yes	No
	_____	Yes	No
5.	_____	Yes	No
	_____	Yes	No
	_____	Yes	No
	_____	Yes	No

See Table 2 in Chapter 4 for example.

FORM 3.   Summary of compliance with commands

Child: _____

Parent(s): _____

Period of data collection: _____

Complete the percentage of compliance for each command on Form 2. Determine the average compliance across the total period of data collection (either baseline or treatment) for each command, and record it on this sheet. For each command that is less than 50% compliance, put a check in the hard commands column.

Command	% Compliance	Hard Command
		(place check)
1.		
2.		
3.		
4.		
5.		
6.		
7.		

See Table 3 in Chapter 4 for example.

FORM 4.   Identified hard commands

Child: _____

Parent(s): _____

Date: _____

Using the information from Form 3, list each of the commands identified as hard.

Command or instruction
1.
2.
3.
4.
5.

FORM 5.   Data sheet for identifying easy commands

Child: _____

Parent(s): _____

Have the parent collect data on possible easy commands you suggested. Use an additional data sheet if tracking more than five commands. The parent writes down the command that was given and whether compliance occurred (by circling C or NC). Determine the percentage of compliance, and then check whether it is an easy command (compliance greater than 75%).

Command	Date	Compliance/ Noncompliance		% Compliance	Easy command (place check)
_____	_____	C	NC		
	_____	C	NC		
	_____	C	NC		
	_____	C	NC		
	_____	C	NC	_____	
_____	_____	C	NC		
	_____	C	NC		
	_____	C	NC		
	_____	C	NC		
	_____	C	NC		
	_____	C	NC		
	_____	C	NC	_____	
_____	_____	C	NC		
	_____	C	NC		
	_____	C	NC		
	_____	C	NC	_____	
_____	_____	C	NC		
	_____	C	NC		
	_____	C	NC		
	_____	C	NC		
	_____	C	NC	_____	
_____	_____	C	NC		
	_____	C	NC		
	_____	C	NC		
	_____	C	NC		
	_____	C	NC	_____	

See Table 3 in Chapter 4 for example.

FORM 6. Targeted hard commands

Child: _____

Age: _____

Date: _____

List two to five hard commands you will target with behavioral momentum.

Commands targeted for behavioral momentum
1.
2.
3.
4.
5.

FORM 7. Suggested easy-to-hard command sequences

Child: _____

Age: _____

Provide several examples of series of three or four easy commands followed by a targeted command for the parents to review and study before implementing behavioral momentum. This can also be rehearsed in session.

Easy command sequence #1
1.
2.
3.
4.
5.

Hard command _____

Easy command sequence #2
1.
2.
3.
4.
5.
Hard command _____

Easy command sequence #3
1.
2.
3.
4.
5.

Hard command _____

Easy command sequence #4
1.
2.
3.
4.
5.

Hard command _____

FORM 8.   Rules for implementing behavioral momentum (for parent)

When using behavioral momentum, remember the following four rules:

1. Get close to the child before issuing the first easy command.
2. The easy command sequence, as well as the following hard command, should be given in rapid sequence.
3. Praise should be given after each complaint response in the easy command sequence and also during the child's compliance with the hard command (to keep compliance going).
4. Following compliance with the hard command, effusive praise and a preferred activity should follow.

FORM 9.   Schedule for embedding easy commands in daily activities

Parent(s):_____

Discuss with the parents some activities during with they will present the child with one of the easy commands each day. List the activity (e.g., mealtime) and several easy commands the parents will present periodically during this activity. Make sure they praise and reinforce compliance with these easy commands.

Activity   **Suggested Embedded Easy Commands**
_____   _____
_____   _____
_____   _____

☐ **Chapter 5**

FORM 1.   Noncompliance barometer with ten units

10
9
8
7
6
5
4
3
2
1

FORM 2.   Noncompliance barometer with fifteen units

15
14
13
12
11
10
9
8
7
6
5
4
3
2
1

FORM 3.   Noncompliance barometer with twenty units

20
19
18
17
16
15
14
13
12
11
10
9
8
7
6
5
4
3
2
1

FORM 4. Fine contingency: Noncompliance barometer

If_____, does not comply according to the following (provide definition of compliance):

_____

_____

_____

Then the barometer is moved down one level. If_____goes below_____level, he or she loses the designated reinforcer.

FORM 5. Compliance barometer

When giving a command or request, make sure you follow these four steps:
1. You are within arm's length of the child before delivering the command.
2. You gain your child's attention.
3. You present a clear statement regarding the behavior or performance expected.
4. You issue the request or command once.

☐ **Chapter 6**

FORM 1.   Interview sheet for assessing the severity of a child's school-related behavior problem

---

1. Has the child been sent home for a behavioral incident? If yes, how many times? Describe the incidents that resulted in suspension or expulsion.
2. Is the child's behavior a source of concern to the teacher? Has such behavior been brought up as a concern during parent-teacher conferences? You may need to speak with the teacher about his or her concerns if parents consent to disclosure of information.)
3. Has the teacher requsted that the parent consult a physician on the possible appropriateness of medications designed to manage child's behavior? (This should be a warning sign that all is not well in the classroom.)
4. Have the parents been asked to consent to assessment to determine the child's eligibility for special education services, required in some degree by the problem behaviors demonstrated in the regular classroom?
5. Do the parents feel they need some way to impress their child with the importance of good behavior at school? Have other attempts by the parents to promote good behavior been ineffective? Has counseling been rendered and have been found not to result in a behavior change in a school?

See Table 1 in Chapter 6 for example.

FORM 2.   Parent-school agreement of targeted behavior to the tracked for daily report card

---

Student: _____

Date: _____

In Section I, list the problem behaviors (ones that you wish to decrease) to be tracked (if any). In section II, list the appropriate behavior (that you wish to increase) to be tracked (if any). The specific tracking form to be used can be taken from Chapter 2 forms.

Problem behaviors to be tracked
1.
2.
3.
Appropriate behaviors to be tracked
1.
2.
3.
Signatures
Teacher _____
Principal _____
Parent _____
Parent _____
Clinician _____
See Table 3 in Chapter 6 for example.

FORM 3.   Possible privileges to be earned or lost in daily report card system

---

Child: _____

Possible privileges to earn daily
Extra TV, videos, Nintendo
Special breakfast of child's choice (e.g., pancakes instead of just cereal)
Later bedtime
Less homework (if teacher agrees)
Getting out of one or more chores
Money (almost always assured to be a powerful event)
Possible privileges to earn Weekly
Trip to mall
Trip to swimming pool
No Saturday afternoon chores
Video rental of choice on Friday or Saturday night
Special outing
Money
Agreed-on privileges to be earned
Daily
Weekly

FORM 4.   Behavioral agreement: Daily report card

If_____does the following behavior(s):

1. _____ _____ (designate levels of occurrence)
2. _____ _____ (designate levels of occurrence)

at the designated levels, then he or she earns the following daily or weekly privileges:

_____

_____

_____

☐ **Chapter 7**

FORM 1. Screening questions for child disruptive behavior

Have the parent place a check next to each that applies.

_____ Does the child engage in disruptive behavior during unstructured or play periods? If so, what specific behaviors:
      _____ Tantrums
      _____ Throws toys
      _____ Aggressive against other children
      _____ Does not wait for own turn
      _____ Runs inside areas
      _____ Other

_____ Do you find yourself frequently intervening during the child's play to stop his or her disruptive behavior?

_____ Do you feel ineffective in supervising your child's play?

_____ Is your child's disruptive behavior more frequent or severe than other children's behaviors?

FORM 2. Situations in which not to use time-out

1. Child is to do chores (when he or she dislikes doing the particular chore).
2. Child is supposed to be doing homework.
3. Child is supposed to be getting ready for bed.
4. Child is a picky eater during mealtime.

FORM 3.   Brief program write-up for time-out

Child: _____

Parent(s): _____

Date: _____

1. Targeted behavior that results in time-out:

2. Minimum length of time-out period:

3. Time-out area:

4. Release criteria from time-out (what most children do before getting out of time-out):

5. Behavior(s) to be praised after release from time-out:

FORM 4.   Seven mistakes in using time-out

1. Time-out is not consistently used for one or two targeted behaviors only.
2. The target behaviors often occur without the parents following through.
3. No designated specific length for time-out.
4. Time-out area is near toys or entertainment.
5. Child is not supervised while in time-out.
6. Child is not required to remain in time-out area for minimum time length. (i.e., gets up frequently or leaves time-out area unauthorized).
7. Release from time-out is done at a time when child is engaged in tantrum or disruptive behavior (in the time-out area).

FORM 5.   Questions for parents on use of time-out

1. What if your child gets out of the time-out seat?
2. What if he or she screams while in time-out?
3. What if he or she apologizes while in time-out and then asks to get out?
4. What if your child gets out of the time-out seat and then refuses to go back to it?
5. What if your child begins to play with a toy nearby while in time-out?

Answers appear in text at the end of Chapter 7.

☐ **Chapter 8**

FORM 1.   Parent questionnaire: Shopping trips

Have the parent place a check next to each one that applies.

_____ Does your child wander off to other parts of the store while you are shopping?

_____ Does your child repeatedly call out to you?

_____ Does your child ask or beg you to buy items that are not on the shopping list?

_____ Does your child display poor public manners during shopping trips?

_____ Does your child argue or fight with siblings during shopping trips?

_____ Does your child play tag or other roughhouse games while in the store?

_____ Does your child touch merchandise on the shelves or in the display cases?

_____ Does your child scream of cry excessively during shopping trips?

_____ Do you dread taking your child on a shopping trip?

_____ Are there behaviors that occur that have not been listed above? If so, specify:

_____

_____

_____

FORM 2.   Parent handout for guidelines for acceptable child behavior

Stay close to the shopping cart.
The child should be within arm's length of the parent, the shopping cart, or a sibling who is touching the cart.

Make no distracting remarks.
The child should not argue with the parents or siblings, tease siblings, or repeatedly call out to either. He or she should not beg, ask, or demand that the parents buy something not on the shopping list or request to go into another section of the store.

Display good manners.
Yelling, fighting, roughhousing, hanging all over the cart, playing tag, playing other games, and excessive whining or crying are not permitted.

Do no touch the store merchandise.
The child should not pick up any of the items on the shelves, display cases, or aisle displays.

FORM 3.   Shopping stipend card

Rule Violation		Frequency				
Not close to cart	1	2	3	4	5	6
Distracting remarks	1	2	3	4	5	6
Bad manners	1	2	3	4	5	6
Touching merchandise	1	2	3	4	5	6

See Table 4 in Chapter 8 for example.

☐ **Chapter 9**

FORM 1. Parent questionnaire interview for dining-out experience
---

Section I. Distress level
Rate the following questions on a 1 to 9 scale using the anchor points below:

1	**3**	**7**	**9**
Never	Seldom	Often	Always

_____ Do you have to remind your child to behave appropriately while in a restaurant?

_____ Does your child behave in a manner that embarrasses you?

_____ Do you postpone or avoid going out to eat primarily for reasons involving your child's behavior in the restaurant?

_____ Do you feel as if there is nothing you can do to control the situation?

Section II. Types of problem
The following questions can be used to get an idea of the types of problem behaviors parents encounter during dinner excursions. Next to each item, indicate whether the behavior never occurs (N), occurs on some trips but not all (S), occurs every trip (E), or occurs multiple times during each trip (MT).

_____ Plays with utensils, napkins, glasses

_____ Leaves table without permission

_____ Argue or fight with sibling(s)

_____ Throws tantrums

_____ Throws food

Section III. General information
1. What strategies have you used to get your child to behave more appropriately during restaurant outings?
2. Are the problems displayed during restaurant outings typical or atypical of the child's behavior? In other words, do you have problems with the child's behavior just during restaurant outings, or are their other times or places where inappropriate or disruptive behavior is a problem?
3. Do you have any other comments that have not been covered by previous questions?

FORM 2.   Specific components of family advice package

1. Specify appropriate child behavior for the restaurant.
2. Locate a table or booth away from the crowd.
3. Seat the children on the inside, next to the wall.
4. Separate the children.
5. Provide the children with a premeal snack.
6. Order food that the children enjoy.
7. Provide small, interesting toys to occupy their time.
8. Move the dinner utensils from the children's reach during the premeal time.
9. Remove the toys when the food arrives.
10. Periodically praise the children for appropriate behavior or provide a point system.

Note. From "Dining out with children: Effectiveness of a parent advice package on pre-meal inappropriate behavior," by K. E. Bauman, M. L. Reiss, R. W. Rogers, & J. S. Bailey, 1983, *Journal of Applied Behavior Analysis, 16,* p. 55–68.

FORM 3.   Appropriate child dining behavior

Talking in an appropriate conversational tone
Making a request in an acceptable vocal manner
Sitting in the chair
Keeping the hands and feet to oneself
Using utensils appropriately
Eating food appropriately

FORM 4.   Inappropriate behaviors during dining (with fine system)

1. *Inappropriate verbal behavior,* including crying, whining, demanding, interrupting others, humming, and singing
2. *Inappropriate motor behavior,* including standing on a chair, being out of the chair without permission, hitting or kicking others, and reaching more than halfway across the table
3. *Inappropriate use of food or utensils,* including picking up nonfinger foods with hands, playing with dinner utensils, and stuffing, dropping, or tossing food into the mouth
4. *Noncompliance* with a parental request

Child: _____
Stipend amount: _____
Amount of fine: _____for each occurrence
Date: _____
Restaurant: _____

1. Inappropriate verbal behavior	1	2	3	4	5
2 Inappropriate motor behavior	1	2	3	4	5
3. Inappropriate use of utensils	1	2	3	4	5
4. Noncompliance	1	2	3	4	5

Balance _____

INDEX